THE INSIDER'S GUIDE TO
J·A·P·A·N

THE INSIDER'S GUIDES
JAPAN • CHINA • KOREA • HAWAII • HONG KONG • AUSTRALIA

The Insider's Guide to Japan
First published 1985
revised and updated 1987
Merehurst Press
5 Great James Street
London WC1N 3DA
by arrangement with CFW Publications Ltd

© 1987 CFW Publications Ltd

ISBN: 0 948075 18 X

Created, edited and produced by CFW Publications Ltd
130 Connaught Road C., Hong Kong
Editor in Chief: Allan Amsel
Design: Hon Bing-wah/Kinggraphic
Text and artwork composed and information updated
on an NBI System 5000 computer

ACKNOWLEDGEMENTS
The author would like to thank the many friends who, knowingly or
unknowingly, have made their mark on this book.
He feels particularly indebted to Mr Hiroshi Ishikawa of the
Foreign Press Center, Tokyo, and the staff of
the Tourist Information Center, Tokyo,
for their generous assistance.

CREDITS
Photo of Cinderella's Castle, Tokyo Disneyland, on page 96
(c) Walt Disney Productions Inc. Photo by Tim Porter.

EDITOR'S NOTE
The names of Meiji and pre-Meiji Japanese are given in the Japanese order,
with the surname first; names of post-Meiji Japanese are given
in the Western order.

Printed in Korea

THE INSIDER'S GUIDE TO

JAPAN

by Peter Popham

Photographed by Nik Wheeler

MEREHURST PRESS
— LONDON —

Contents

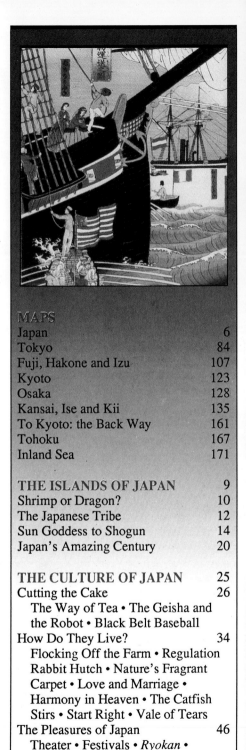

J·A·P·A·N

--- · --- Shinkansen ——————— Railways

0 50 100 200 300 400 500

km

KYUSHU · Kagoshima

EAST CHINA SEA

NANSEI ISLANDS

Okinawa Island
· Naha

Iriomote
National Park
Ishigaki Island

HONSHU

ISHIKAWA
Hakui ·

Kanazawa ·
TOYAM
Chubu-Sanga
National Park

· Masuda
SHIMANE   TOTTORI   Miyazu   Fukui · Takayama
Hagi ·   Bay   FUKUI
· Tsuwano   Tottori ·   Tsuruga   NA
Shimonoseki Ogori YAMAGUCHI Hiroshima CHUGOKU Amanohashidate   CHUBU
Fukuoka   ·   HIROSHIMA OKAYAMA HYOGO SHIGA   Gifu ·
(Hakata)   Kitakyushu Miyajima Onomichi Okayama Kurashiki Himeji KYOTO Lake GIFU
SAGA   FUKUOKA   Shodo Island Mt.Rokko Biwa   · Nagoya
NAGASAKI   OITA   Imabari · Inland Sea Marugame   Kobe · Kyoto   AICHI
·Nagasaki Beppu   Matsuyama ·   Takamatsu Osaka· Nara
Unzen-Amakusa Kumamoto · Aso   Kotohira KAGAWA
National Park   Mt. Aso EHIME   KOCHI   Tokushima NARA MIE
Amakusa   Uwajima ·   TOKUSHIMA   KINKI Ise · Toba Hamamatsu
Islands   KUMAMOTO   Kochi ·   SH
KAGOSHIMA MIYAZAKI · Hyuga SHIKOKU   WAKAYAMA
                                              Kii Peninsula
Kagoshima · Mt. Takachino   KYUSHU
Sakurajima Island · Miyazaki
Ibusuki · Shibushi
Mt. Kaimon

HOKKAIDO

Daisetsuzan
National Park

Shikotsu-Toya · Sapporo   Akan National Park
National Park
Noboribetsu Spa   · Akankokan
Lake Toya   Lake Shikotsu   Lake Kutcharo
                                  Lake Akan
· Tomakomai
Noboribetsu

SEA OF JAPAN

· Aomori

AOMORI

AKITA   IWATE
Akita **TOHOKU**
· Morioka

YAMAGATA

▲ Mt. Haguro

Sado Island   ▲ Mt. Gasson   **MIYAGI**
                               · Ayukawa
Niigata   · Ojika Peninsula
               ▲ Mt. Bandai   Matsushima
                               Sendai Kinkazan
                                       Island
NIIGATA   · Fukushima

GUMMA   Nikko·   **FUKUSHIMA**
Matsumoto   Lake Chuzenji
hichibu-Tama   Mashiko
ational Park   **TOCHIGI**   · Tsukuba
SAITAMA   **IBARAKI**
s   **KANTO**
Izu ▲ Mt. Mitake
k Hakone   Tokyo·   · Narita
awara Yokohama   **CHIBA**
imoda Atami Kamakura
eninsula Oshima **KANAGAWA**
          Island

PACIFIC OCEAN

The
Islands
of
Japan

How big is Japan?

Economically, industrially, even militarily, Japan is one of the world's great powers. Routinely described as a Western country and included in Western counsels, she has climbed from the humiliation and poverty of the post-war years to a position where almost no one in the world is unaffected by what she does and makes.

Yet a glance at the map shows that this power and energy is concentrated

in a country of puny dimensions, a slim string of islands arranged in an arc more than 160 kilometers (100 miles) of stormy sea from the nearest point on the Asian continent. The Japanese themselves, both in pride and exasperation, have traditionally regarded their country as small and remote, contrasting it with the vastness and centrality of China. The modern novelist Yukio Mishima, looking at a map in which Japan was colored pink, was reminded of a shrimp hanging off the underbelly of Asia.

But this isn't the whole story either. Though her slimness would belie it, in area Japan is larger than most of the countries of Europe -- roughly 1-1/2 times the size of the United Kingdom, for example. A large proportion of that area, perhaps 80 per cent, is taken up by densely forested and precipitous mountains and is in consequence very sparsely inhabited. But within the remaining 20 per cent, which consists of coastal plains, narrow river valleys and a few basins in the mountains, is crammed a huge population numbering more than 121,000,000 people, making these zones among the most densely populated in the world. As the perspective changes, the image alters once again, and again we are confronted with a giant: Japan's population is the seventh largest in the world.

These are some of the paradoxes that constitute Japan, a country where neither mountain nor sea is ever far away, where the primeval beauty of the alpine ranges, the forests and the many volcanoes contrasts vividly with the meticulously cultivated paddy fields and the cheerful congestion of the great cities in the plains.

There are great variations of climate in Japan, both from season to season and from place to place. The narrow archipelago stretches from latitude 43° north to about latitude 28° north, with the result that while in March and April the people in the northwest of the country are still shivering in the tail-end of their bitter, snowy winter, the lucky inhabitants of the southern islands are dusting off their bathing suits. Congenially mild, sunny weather is to be found somewhere in the country at almost any time of the year. And although the famous cherry blossoms are only at their best in any one place for a few brief days, by traveling gradually northward the dedicated *sakura* fiend could extend his pleasure to a full six weeks, from the end of March to the middle of May.

ABOVE LEFT The Emperor, the Empress and their immediate family greet their subjects from behind bullet-proof glass every 29 April, the Emperor's birthday. RIGHT Cherry blossoms, Japan's other symbol, at Lake Okutama, west of Tokyo. Their evanescence is part of their appeal.

For those who prefer to stay in one place, there is the subtle and unending spectacle of Japan's changing seasons to be enjoyed. The way some Japanese talk you would think their country had a monopoly on the four seasons; yet there is a regularity to their rotation, and a distinctness to the changes they bring in train, which is very special if not actually unique and which has etched itself deep into the Japanese psyche.

Mild spring, sunny and windy, is succeeded towards the end of June by a month-long rainy season. While it doesn't rain continuously, the downpour can go on for days at a time, and the humidity is high.

Summer is hot and close, uncomfortably so in the low-lying cities. Heavy work schedules prevent city-dwellers in Japan from fleeing in the manner of Parisians and New Yorkers, but they escape when they can and visitors are advised to do likewise. Both mountain and seaside resorts offer a great deal of relief from the heat.

Towards the end of summer, typhoons roar in from the southwest, but generally blow themselves out before reaching Tokyo. Then follow the cloudless skies and gorgeous colors of autumn. Winter, too, is a remarkably dry, bright season, and though snowfall is heavy on the Japan Sea side of the country, on the Pacific side there is little snow and the temperature rarely drops much below freezing.

For the visitor from more insipid climes it is the strongly defined character of the seasons which amazes. The rain, when it rains, is harder and more unrelenting than anything he has ever experienced, and the summer sun hotter; the periods of crystal-clear autumn weather so perfect and prolonged he feels as if he has woken up in heaven.

Accommodating themselves to the dramatically different demands of these seasons, eking a living from the narrow plains, gazing up at the beautiful, unyielding mountains are a people who, despite their huge numbers, are in many ways more like a tribe than the citizens of a nation-state -- the Japanese.

THE JAPANESE TRIBE

Before the last Ice Age Japan was attached to the Asian continent and, like their Korean and Chinese neighbors, the Japanese are a Mongoloid people. Korea is the nearest point to Japan on the continent and always provided the most convenient jumping-off point for migrants and travelers. Certain elements of the culture, such as the flimsiness of the early wooden architecture, suggest that there was an early influx of migrants from more southerly regions, but no archaeological evidence to support this has been discovered.

The picture is complicated by the Ainu, the hairy hunting and fishing tribespeople who until the eighth century occupied the northern part of the main island of Honshu. They were pushed further and further northwards by the dominant Yamato Japanese and as a distinct people exist now only in small communities in the northernmost island of Hokkaido. However, large numbers of them have probably been absorbed over the centuries, as is attested by the bushy eyebrows and deep-set eyes of some of the Japanese today.

The salient fact is that large-scale immigration to Japan had come to a halt by the eighth or ninth century. Since that time -- soon after the dawn of the nation's recorded history -- the Japanese have been, and have regarded themselves as, a single, unified and homogeneous people. With the exception of the arrival of some half million Koreans earlier this century, as slave workers in the Japanese war effort, nothing has occurred during the intervening millennium to disrupt that state of affairs. When a Japanese describes himself as belonging to a single huge family, he has over 1,000 years of history to back him up.

The main reason for this is the country's geographical situation, in which it is arguable that the Japanese have been uniquely fortunate. They were never too far from the Asian mainland to get there when they really needed to, and generations of priests and scholars made the journey to China and Korea

fleet before he could inflict serious damage.

Later, in the seventeenth century, when the intentions of the Western missionaries and merchants who had established a foothold in the country aroused the suspicions of the military ruler, the encircling seas enabled him to draw a curtain of isolation around Japan almost without effort, and this state lasted for 250 years.

Blessed with the fruits of China's civilization but spared the bloody turmoil of her history, the Japanese have been, until their modern century, the

and back, bringing all those elements, practical and spiritual, of the culture of China which enabled Japan to attain a high level of civilization. But the journey was long and hazardous. Even the shortest route was more than four times the distance from Dover to Calais, while the distance to China was 520 kilometers (450 miles).

This long and stormy stretch of water acted as a highly effective deterrent to both would-be migrants and invaders. The only general to challenge it was the Mongol conqueror Kublai Khan, who sent a great armada to invade Japan in the thirteenth century. A providential typhoon, dubbed 'kami-kaze' or 'divine wind' by the Japanese, destroyed his

most isolated and the most homogeneous of the world's great peoples. This has given them both the strengths and the weaknesses of a tribe. The strengths are a close identification of the individual with his people, the social harmony this brings and a great capacity for concerted effort. Weaknesses that one might point to would include the low priority given to the development and free expression of individual personality, the potential for nationalistic egotism which welled up during the years before the last war and a deep uncer-

British soldiers march along The Bluff in Yokohama past the British Legation, preceeded by a military band, in a late 18th century print.

tainty about how to get along with the outside world.

Although Japan has been a member of the international community for more than 100 years now, these strengths and weaknesses continue to manifest themselves in both individual and national behavior. Alert visitors will be quick to notice them.

However, they will be even quicker to notice two other characteristics of the Japanese: their kindness and generosity. Lost, even in the middle of Tokyo, you can expect to be guided gently on your way; caught in a storm

without an umbrella, you will frequently find one is hoisted above you. People who have tried hitchhiking report that drivers will go hours or even days out of their way to help them. And if you get a chance to spend time with a family or to visit a spot in the country where foreigners do not usually venture, you will be overwhelmed by the warm, thoughtful and solicitous welcome.

ABOVE Part of Kiyomizu Temple, one of Kyoto's most magnificent. CENTER Early (1861) Japanese depiction of an Englishman on horseback.

SUN GODDESS TO SHOGUN

It is probable that the Japanese arrived in their archipelago from Korea, but according to national myth they descended from heaven.

The grandson of the sun goddess, commanded to rule the country, arrived on Mt. Takachiho, a volcano which is still active in the southern island of Kyushu. It was the great-grandson of this god, the story goes, who became the first earthly emperor of Japan. He established the seat of his power in the plain of Yamato in the main island, Honshu, perhaps around the beginning of the Christian era, and his descendants have reigned (though rarely ruled) ever since.

Whatever the historical facts, this story has served the imperial family well. The emperor's supposedly divine origins meant that in the early centuries

he was both the secular and spiritual ruler of his people. His secular power disappeared quite early on, but his holiness and the mythical link to the origins of his people ensured his survival. For long centuries the imperial family lived in powerless obscurity in Kyoto, but they were never threatened with extinction. And, as we shall see, they made an amazing comeback at the start of Japan's modern era. They are by a long way the oldest royal family in the world.

Yamato, the first emperor's base, is a plain in Kinki, the region which includes the modern cities of Kyoto, Osaka and Nara. Huge earth mounds dot this plain, marking the graves of Japan's prehistoric leaders. Pottery found with the mounds suggests that these earliest decendants of the sun goddess were horse-riding, sword-toting warriors, and forerunners of the samurai.

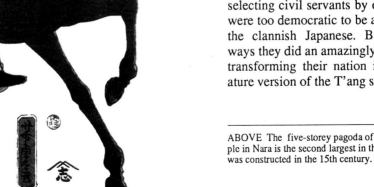

During the early centuries of the Christian era, contact between Japan and the continent was frequent, and Chinese influence continually seeped into the country. But during the sixth century, as China approached her glorious T'ang period, this influence became suddenly and dramatically stronger.

Buddhism, the Indian religion which the Chinese had made their own, was one of the early imports and brought much art, architecture and learning in rain. Also important was the model of centralized government, and the code of

law and system of taxation which went with it. Some Chinese ways were unsuited to the Japanese situation and faded away once the initial enthusiasm gave out. Others, such as the system of selecting civil servants by examination, were too democratic to be acceptable to the clannish Japanese. But in many ways they did an amazingly good job of transforming their nation into a miniature version of the T'ang state.

ABOVE The five-storey pagoda of Kofukuji Temple in Nara is the second largest in the country. It was constructed in the 15th century.

And as Japan was spared the waves of invasion which rolled across China, flattening her early achievements, Japan is the best place to see the architectural and artistic styles of the T'ang today. The city of Nara, laid out in 710, was the country's first 'permanent' capital (though it only lasted as a capital for 70-odd years). The temples and monasteries in the pleasant parkland at the city's old center reflect the purity of the Chinese influence at this time, and the fabulous achievement of the Japanese carpenters in mastering the foreign techniques.

T'ang dynasty was past its best by this time, and after three centuries of imitation the Japanese had gained enough confidence in their own abilities to go it alone. So from this time the Chinese influence began to dwindle, and in its

Nara was abandoned for reasons unknown, and the reigning emperor decided to build a new capital called Heian-kyo (present-day Kyoto) a little further to the north. Like Nara, Heian was laid out like a chessboard in imitation of the Chinese capital Ch'ang-an, and this street-plan is still intact today. The city was to remain the nation's capital, at least in name, right up to 1868.

Heian-kyo was founded in 794. The

place blossomed the culture of the Heian court.

Heian means 'peace' and the Heian period was indeed a blessedly peaceful interlude. The imperial court, in accordance with Chinese practice, was supposed to be the center of government, but quite rapidly control devolved to local clan leaders throughout the country. This left the court with plenty of wealth but very little to do except enact the empty ceremonies of power. The rest of the time they plotted, made love, dashed off countless poems, held elegant contests of aesthetic sensitivity and wrote diaries. The world's first novel, *The Tale of Genji* written at that

ABOVE RIGHT Devotees in Todaiji Temple, Nara, home of the nation's largest Great Buddha. CENTER Outlandish-looking members of an early Japanese delegation, photographed in Honolulu. *Photo courtesy of the Mainichi Shimbun-Sha.*

16

time by the woman courtier Murasaki Shikibu, paints an unforgettably vivid picture of this foppish age.

The Heian court was clearly too soft to last. The descendants of younger sons of the aristocracy, who had been sent into the countryside from the capital in earlier days, gradually acquired military as well as political power, and increasingly the most powerful of these tough, frugal warriors were called on by the court to protect them from gangs of armed Buddhist monks who had begun to terrorize the capital. Two principal families, the Genji and the Heike, competed for this role of guardian, and before long they were fighting each other as well.

Two major explosions followed. The second and decisive one shattered what was left of the court's authority and left the country in the hands of the leader of the Genji clan, a fierce young warrior called Minamoto Yoritomo. He established his capital hundreds of miles from Kyoto in the obscure but easily defended fishing village of Kamakura, south of present-day Yokohama.

The culture of the Kamakura period which ensued, lasting for the next century and a half, was a harsh and earthy contrast to that of the Heian court. But whereas the Heian period is utterly strange to modern Japanese, during the Kamakura period there came into being many of the ideas and values which have governed the people's minds ever since.

We could call it the age of the cultured warrior. Unlike his medieval European counterparts, the Kamakura samurai did not despise learning, and, when Zen Buddhism was introduced from China at the start of this era, he recognized in its simplicity of expression and its stress on self-discipline and exertion as a way of attaining enlightenment the perfect complement to his Spartan military lifestyle. If the Heian period was like a hot, perfumed bath, the culture produced by this union of warrior and monk was as bracing as an icy shower.

This fruitful relationship between Zen and the Japanese ruling class continued for hundreds of years, far beyond the Kamakura period, and left its mark on many different aspects of the culture, from the tea ceremony and *tatami* mats to garden design and flower-arranging.

Meanwhile Buddhism was enjoying a boom among the lower classes too, as new Japanese sects sprang up, offering salvation through the endless repetition of devotional phrases. With their emphasis on personal salvation in a literal heaven, some of these sects bear a closer resemblance to Christianity than to Buddhism as practiced in other parts of Asia. They owed much of their success to the political and economic confusion at the start of the period.

The Kamakura shoguns survived the Mongolian menace at the end of the thirteenth century, but the structural weakness of their administration, based on the loyalty of a few chieftains spread throughout the country, gradually began to tell. When the quixotic Emperor Godaigo (1288-1339) attempted to seize power by force of arms, the regime succumbed. Godaigo had no great success, but his attempt ushered in an era of war and confusion which lasted more than 200 years.

Central authority and the old estate divisions broke down during these years. As strong warrior chiefs, some from old aristocratic families but many of common descent, forced their way to power and then, as *daimyo* (feudal lords) staked out rational and readily defensible domains, Japan became a patchwork quilt of tiny fiefdoms. And as they consolidated their rule, candidates for top dog began to emerge.

This process was hastened by the arrival in Japan of the first Europeans. Approaching the country from the south, and dubbed for that reason 'southern barbarians', the Portuguese arrived in Japan in 1543. They amazed the natives by their appearance and their manners, and delighted them with their tobacco, sponge cake, clocks and spectacles; but it was their harquebuses which left the deepest mark on Japanese history.

The military value of firepower was rapidly grasped, and within 20 years cannons and muskets were being widely and decisively used in battle. Only the richer of the *daimyo* could afford to employ the new technology and to put up the monumental new castles which were the only effective type of defense against it. The struggle for power between the *daimyo* suddenly accelerated. Before the end of the sixteenth century, a resolution had been reached which was to last until the arrival of the next wave of destructive technology from the West 300 years later.

Clambering out of the smoke of battle into the center of the picture came three great generals, one after the other. Between them they crushed or won over all who opposed them, unified the country politically and ushered in a long age of authoritarian calm which is one of the wonders of world history.

The first, Oda Nobunaga, was a ferocious man, and one of the main objects of his ferocity was the Buddhist armies which had gained great power during the previous chaotic century. The enmity he had for them encouraged him to favour the Portuguese Jesuit missionaries, led by St. Francis Xavier, who had begun introducing Christianity into the country. For many years they enjoyed great success, converting as many as 300,000 Japanese to the faith until, losing favour with a later shogun, they and their works were stamped out and Christianity effectively disappeared from the country.

Hideyoshi, the second and most interesting of the three, was a small and famously ugly man who rose to supremacy from the rank of foot-soldier. He was a general of Alexandrian ambition: in an attempt to conquer China he had his troops overrun Korea, thereby poisoning the feelings of the Koreans towards the Japanese for good. But he was also an administrator of genius, balancing the forces of antagonistic and loyal *daimyo* throughout the nation to ensure the stability of his rule. In order to prevent other ambitious soldiers from treading in his footsteps he drew a strict and largely artificial line between samurai and commoners, and issued laws preventing members of different classes from changing their professions.

The third general, Tokugawa Ieyasu, who lived from 1542 to 1616, is remembered for his patience and his cunning, and also for his fantastically gaudy mausoleum at Nikko which illustrates how drastically the taste of the Japanese ruling class had changed since the somber tranquillity of the Kamakura period. Tokugawa consolidated the work of his predecessors. He pre-empted opposition to his rule by insisting that *daimyo* spend alternate years at home and at his capital in Edo (modern Tokyo), thus wasting much time and money on the road, and by keeping their wives as permanent hostages in Edo.

He also skillfully arranged for the succession to stay in his family, and the Tokugawas ruled Japan, at least in name, from 1603 to 1868. For all but the earliest years of that period the only contact Japan maintained with the Western world was through a tiny Dutch trading settlement on an artificial island in Nagasaki Harbor.

There is a repressive quality about the long Tokugawa years which is

18

deeply unattractive. Every aspect of the citizen's life, from his occupation and thesize and design of his house to the style of his hair and clothes, was dictated bythe government with the objective of freezing the social structure in place to ensure political stability.

So it is paradoxical that this period was in fact a time of great change and growth. The merchant class in particular, theoretically at the bottom of the social scale, grew enormously in wealth, and a whole new culture, flamboyant and frivolous, sprang up to entertain it. Most of those forms by which the rest of the world defines the word 'Japanese'-- *kabuki*, geisha, woodblock prints, for example -- were part of that great surge of mercantile confidence.

And however unpleasant the means by which it was brought about, the long peace was a great blessing. While nothing resembling an industrial revolution took place, craftsmanship in many different fields attained an extraordinarily high level which is still reflected in much present-day work. The standard of living of the common people rose and education, provided by schools in temples, improved to the extent that about 35 per cent of the population was literate by the nineteenth century.

Though deprived of the scientific advances enjoyed in the West, the Japanese were spared the humiliation and exploitation of colonialism. They survived, although blinkered and ill-informed, with pride and national integrity intact. When the shogunate -- a very ripe fruit by the end -- finally fell, the Japanese were, among Asian peoples, uniquely ready to take up the challenges of the modern world.

JAPAN'S AMAZING CENTURY

In 1854, under the threat of force from the American Navy, Japan grudgingly

---

Industry and shipping at Yokohama Port, the nation's largest trading port.

opened her doors to trade with the West. Six years later the first Japanese embassy was sent to Washington. A photograph survives from that mission: the ambassadors, posing with American naval officers and dressed in their samurai finery -- split-toed socks, divided skirts, kimonos, shaved scalps and topknots, and two swords each -- look wildly outlandish. Their befuddled, faraway expressions convey deep culture shock. They are obviously unaccustomed to sitting on chairs. No delegation of painted Papuan tribesmen could look more exotic or more distant from the modern world.

Yet less than 70 years later the grandsons of these men, dressed in collars and ties, were to sit across the table from the world's great powers and participate with them on terms of perfect equality in the peace conference which ended World War I -- the only non-Western power to do so.

The transformation was close to miraculous. How did it happen?

In a sense it was a re-enactment, 1,200 years later and under radically different conditions, of Japan's experience with China. In both cases, recognizing her backwardness *vis-a-vis* the other country or countries, she set about learning with fierce determination what was necessary to even the score.

Japan's initial feeling towards the new intruders was quite simply revulsion, and anger with the weak shogunate for letting them in. People remembered the emperor again -- 'Honor the emperor and expel the barbarian!' was the popular slogan.

But once the shogun had been deposed and the emperor restored to his former glory (though as usual he had very little real power) in the new capital of Tokyo, things changed. The barbarian would not go away, and he was far too strong to be pushed out. Furthermore, some of his inventions -- lightning conductors, steam engines and cannons, for example -- were genuinely useful. A new slogan, 'A rich country and a strong military', was adopted, and the new government, composed of young and highly enterprising samurai from the southwest, set about implementing it with fantastic dispatch.

The eagerness to learn which Japan demonstrated during the last third of the nineteenth century contrasts starkly with the pride and the stubborn adherence to tradition which characterized China during the period. Carefully choosing the most appropriate teacher for each subject, the Japanese learned avidly how to build a modern army and navy, a railway network, a textile industry, how to create an education system, a law code, a constitution. Cheerfully discarding their own 'primitive' culture, they hurried to embrace the accessories of Western civilization -- Western clothes, Western music, ballroom dancing... .

No country in history had experienced such a rapid and drastic transformation. The period was crowned by two victories in war against gigantic opponents: China in 1895 and Russia in 1905. These amazed the world, not only because Japan won, but because of the civilized way in which the Japanese treated prisoners and civilians, a striking contrast to their behavior in World War II. Japan became the first Asian nation to be admitted as an equal to the counsels of the rich industrial nations -- and she remains the only one, even to this day.

Among the lessons Japan learned was parliamentary democracy. She applied this thoroughly alien concept with great care and caution, and the power of elected politicians was always checked in the early days by the strength of the military leaders and the 'elder statesmen', founders of the new regime, who kept a keen, corrective eye on their juniors.

As the last of these elder statesmen

died out in the early 1920s and politicians who were neither soldiers nor aristocrats rose to high office for the first time, there was an interval of calm and moderation which suggested to the optimistic that a peaceful, democratic future awaited the country. A new modern literature blossomed. The prince regent -- the present emperor -- traveled to Europe, the first member of the imperial family to leave the country, and came back with a lasting love of oatmeal and golf.

By the end of the decade and with the onset of the Depression, however, people realized this pleasant prospect was a mirage. During the next ten years the system collapsed, undermined by corruption and weakness within and violent insubordination without. Angry and self-righteous young army officers, fiercely patriotic, repeatedly seized the initiative to deepen the nation's military involvement with China and to assassinate balky or pacific politicians.

By 1937 Japan was at war with Chiang Kai-shek in China, and in 1940 she signed the Tripartite Axis Pact with Germany and Italy. In 1941, with no leader strong enough to halt the momentum built up during a decade of reckless and unplanned expansion, she crashed headlong into war with the United States and Great Britain. Despite early successes, the latter half of the war was a long nose-dive towards self-destruction. Perhaps only the sanity of the mild emperor, who took the decision to surrender, prevented the country from being laid to waste altogether.

Even so, the damage was staggering. All the great cities, with the exception of Kyoto, were destroyed. In all, 40 per cent of the built-up area of 60 towns and cities was burnt to the ground. Nearly 700,000 civilians were killed, including 100,000 who died on one night in Tokyo as a result of incendiary bombing. Even Japan's frequent earthquakes had never done damage on this

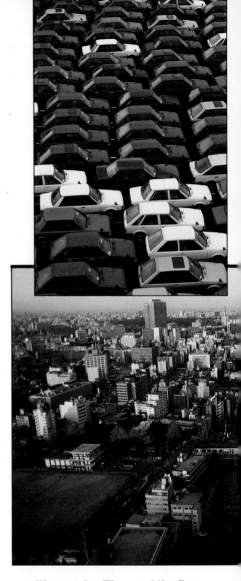

appalling scale. The world's first use of nuclear bombs, dropped on Hiroshima and Nagasaki, completed the carnage.

After the war an Allied army of occupation took over under General MacArthur and ruled Japan until 1952. Under MacArthur's supervision the whole social and economic structure of the country was overhauled. A new constitution sheared the emperor of his divinity, while allowing him to remain a symbol of the nation. Farmers grew rich by means of land reform, and the

22

educational system was remodeled along American lines. An attempt was made to dismantle the *zaibatsu*, the huge financial empires blamed for stoking the war effort. Then MacArthur's priority shifted to the creation of a staunchly anti-communist Japan. Article 9 of the new constitution renounced the use of force for aggressive purposes, and though the article remains in force today it has not prevented the country from re-arming.

Gradually, during the 50s and early 60s, as economic recovery got under way, the old strength and confidence

returned. The Tokyo Olympic Games of 1964, the first ever to be held in Asia, signified that Japan was once again a full member of the community of nations, and the inauguration of the Shinkansen, the fastest train in the world, in the same year gave a hint of the technological prowess with which she has been dazzling the world ever since. Her rapid return to prosperity has been one of the wonders of the post-war age.

The new Japan has been described as a 'fragile super-power', and in terms of her dangerous dependence on distant resources it is a fair description. Socially, however, despite the great changes of the past three decades, Japan remains in extraordinarily good shape. Crime and disaffection are still very low, and the industriousness and homogeneity of the people have been only marginally affected by the new material wealth.

Big problems remain, however. Internationally, the resentment of Japan's huge volume of exports increases every year; at home political corruption is acknowledged to be widespread -- the long-running Lockheed pay-off case reached a climax in 1983 when former prime minister Kakuei Tanaka received an unsuspended four-year prison sentence, against which he is appealing for taking a bribe -- and many Japanese, even among the young, complain that spiritual qualities have been sacrificed in the post-war rush to catch up with the West.

We come back to our original question: how big is Japan? Sometimes the computers, the world-beating auto industry and the robots make her appear a great star in the center of the modern stage. At other times her self-obsession, and her apparent inability, in the field of foreign policy, to do anything but echo America, make her seem only a very curious bit-player right at the edge of things. Only time will tell which of these roles really fits.

TOP Mazda cars lined up waiting to be shipped abroad.
CENTER The crazy concrete of central Tokyo's skyline.

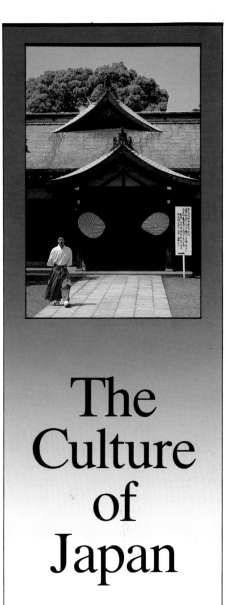

The
Culture
of
Japan

CUTTING THE CAKE

The culture of Japan is rather like a layer cake. The top layer is the rich, gleaming, high-tech surface of the modern nation, borrowed with a meticulous eye for detail from West but increasingly spiced with home-grown refinements. But below this, layer upon layer, are the fruits of nearly 2,000 years of civilization.

Elsewhere, in China or Europe, the new tends to replace what has gone before. Not so in Japan. In this country, which has never undergone a revolution and which until 1945 had never been invaded or occupied, habits, styles, religions or art forms which once gain a foothold cling on for centuries. Many of them are still there for our inspection. Some have been stagnant so long that only the form survives, ancient and leathery and requiring specialized knowledge to enjoy. Others though, while faithful to the original inspiration, retain an amazing vigor.

THE WAY OF TEA

Tea was introduced into Japan, together with Zen Buddhism, in the twelfth century and was used by Zen monks as a way of warding off sleepiness during their long periods of meditation. They brewed and drank it in a formalized and starkly simple manner, and it was this ceremony which was adapted by laymen and became a popular pastime of the upper classes.

Ask an educated Japanese what is the heart of his country's traditional culture and he will probably say the tea ceremony. The tiny three-by-three meter (nine-by-nine feet), gloomy and rustic-looking cottage where the tea ceremony took place was the crucible in which Japanese taste was formed. And although the ceremony was mostly

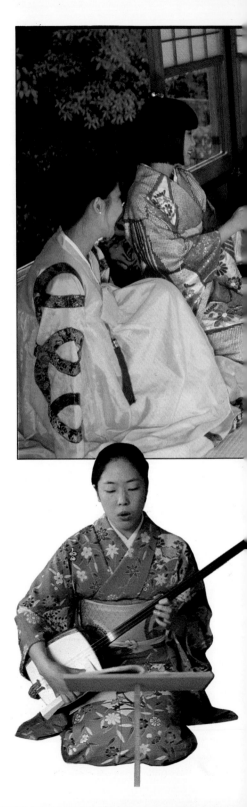

enjoyed by the leisured class, its influence spread everywhere and it is still to be found even in the most garish high street, the humblest home.

If you enjoy the cool touch and green smell of *tatami*, you are appreciating the taste of the tea ceremony. If you find yourself admiring the simple elegance of the old architecture with its quaint and delicate woodwork and paper windows, or the roughness and spontaneity of the old pottery, you are on tea-ceremony wavelength. If you watch a shopkeeper wrap your purchase with deft and nimble fingers, you are witnessing the values the tea ceremony fostered at work.

Yet the tea ceremony was not really a ceremony at all -- it was just a tea party. A small group of friends gathered in surroundings they considered congenial, brewed and drank tea and talked. Great care and discernment went into the choice of everything used at the party: the tea-making utensils and bowls, the tea itself, frothy and bitter, the accompanying cakes, the arrangement of flowers, the scroll hanging on the wall. The conversation, too, was well-considered and tasteful and revolved around the objects used or the beauties of the season. Silence was also permitted.

ABOVE LEFT The tea ceremony, cleverly glamorized for an airline poster and ABOVE RIGHT a *bona fide* tea master. BELOW LEFT A young mistress of traditional *nagauta* singing accompanies herself on the *shamisen*.

The object was to enjoy, in a brief space of time and in simple surroundings, a fragment of eternity; to allow one's true nature, usually buried under noise, activity and desire, to come out and bask in tranquillity.

So there was a spiritual basis to the phenomenon, derived from Buddhism but without any overt religious observance, which is why it is sometimes called 'Zen meditation for laymen'.

The best way to get a feel for tea is simply to notice and relish those things -- *tatami*, pottery and so on -- which it has given to the society at large. Unfortunately the ceremony itself has not only ceased to change but turned slightly sour in its old age. Learning its one thousand and one rules is now one of the main ways a young lady prepares herself for marriage. The naturalness and friendliness which must have played a part have been exorcised, and the ceremony, now truly ceremonious, is performed on stage and presented as if on a velvet cushion for the edification of visiting celebrities as 'the heart of the culture'. It's a pity.

There's a chance it may put down new roots overseas. An American who spent long years studying it in Japan is reported to have developed a new version in which a group of friends gather in congenial surroundings, brew and drink carefully selected coffee and listen to rock music...

THE GEISHA AND THE ROBOT

The hostess-entertainers known as geishas ('art-persons') have excited so much curiosity for so long abroad that many foreigners probably know more about them than most Japanese. A few years ago there were estimated to be 60,000 of them in the country, but it is possible to live here for years and still be very vague about whether they even exist any more. They impinge very lit-

tle on the life of the ordinary person.

The true geisha is a hostess for the big shots. Traditionally and still today, despite the great increase in the number of love marriages, most male entertaining and carousing goes on outside the home and marriage and in the context of work. In Japan business *is* pleasure -- and, conversely, pleasure is very big business. Some 500,000 women are reckoned to be employed in the bars, cabarets, theaters and massage parlors of the capital.

Geishas are at the top of the heap. The 'tea houses' where they operate in the Akasaka, Shimbashi and Yanagibashi quarters of Tokyo are subdued and elegant in the traditional manner. The ladies wear thick white make-up and gorgeous kimonos and have spent many years learning the arts required to soothe the big shots' worried brows: *shamisen* playing, singing, dancing. They are also adept at telling jokes, talking hilariously about nothing much and generally breaking the ice so that the customers, who may be setting up a political deal or negotiating the sale of 100 industrial robots, feel both important enough and comfortable enough to get down to doing business with one another. Many accomplished geishas are more like mothers to their guests than mistresses, but as many as one-third are believed to be 'sponsored' by one or more sugar-daddies. What they do off-stage -- beyond the tea house – may be as important economically as what they do on.

In hot spring resorts and other pleasure zones, as well as in cheaper clubs in the large cities, the line between geisha and call-girl grows very fine.

BLACK BELT BASEBALL

More than any other product of Japanese culture, it is the martial arts which have managed the difficult leap to the outside world.

Judo, 'the way of gentleness' and the most famous, became part of the Olympic Games in 1964 when they were held in Tokyo. **Aikido** and **karate,** too, have soared in popularity in recent years. And **sumo,** the national sport and the only martial art practiced by professionals as well as amateurs, often inspires fanatical enthusiasm in the foreigners who get a chance to see it.

Sumo has been around the longest -- 2,000 years according to some accounts. The history books say a match was first performed before the emperor in AD 100, and his modern descendant maintains the tradition, watching at least one match in Tokyo every year.

Sumo comes as a shock to those who imagine all Japanese to be small and slight. The typical sumo wrestler is an enormous man, tall and fat, who wobbles like jelly whenever he moves. Professionals live out their careers in *heya,* or stables, where a morning of hard training is followed by a hot bath and a huge lunch of meat, fish, *tofu,* vegetables and mountains of rice. The wrestler then snoozes away the afternoon while his meal converts itself happily into fat.

Modern sumo is a brilliant marriage of feudalistic ritual and highly telegenic drama. The elaborate Shinto ceremonies preceding and following the brief bouts have been simplified for the sake of modern audiences without sacrificing the sport's highly exotic flavor.

After several minutes of preparation, during which the combatants stamp, squat, gargle 'Power water' and scatter purifying salt on the clay ring, the bout begins -- and is often over within seconds, with the loser either pushed out of the ring, sometimes somersaulting spectacularly into the arms of those in the front row or forced to touch the ground with some part of his body other than the soles of his feet.

For the newcomer to the sport it may look like nothing more than fat men falling over; the *aficionado* is on the lookout for the skill with which the wrestlers use some of the 70-odd throws, heaves and pushes they are allowed to employ to bring the contest to an end.

Sumo is very popular in Japan and champions are instant celebrities. The huge young Hawaiian Salevaa Atisnoe -- Japanese name Konishiki -- weighs an incredible 219.5 kg. (484 lb.), which makes him the heaviest wrestler in the game's history. The comparatively trim and handsome Chiyonofuji, nicknamed 'Wolf' (*'Urufu'* is how it transliterates into Japanese) is a hero of the day.

Many of the other martial arts date back to the twelfth century when the samurai class first attained real power. Judo, or *jujutsu* as it used to be called, was the art of grappling and flooring an enemy on the battlefield. Like aikido, which was a different branch of the

---

ABOVE LEFT Traditional art and skills survive in many nooks and crannies. Here ladies of Kamakura are instructed in a fan dance.
OVERLEAF Two professional sumo wrestlers prepare to do battle at Yasukuni Shrine.

same art, it was modified in recent times and spread rapidly around the world. Aikido, the less aggressive of the two, depends on disabling an opponent by exerting pain holds on his vital points, then throwing him or pinning him down.

Kendo, 'the way of the sword', is the samurai art *par excellence*. Combatants use bamboo staves in place of swords, wear protectors on the face and other parts on the body, and win by hitting the opponent's head, trunk or wrist or by jabbing him in the throat. It's possible to identify a kendo *dojo* (training hall) from some distance away, due to the feudalistic bellowing and screaming that issues from it.

Quite a number of other arts have survived from that early age. **Kyudo**, Japanese archery, was the subject of a famous book, *Zen in the Art of Archery*. **Yabusame** is archery on horseback, still exhibited regularly at Hachimangu Shrine in Kamakura, near Tokyo (see the**Festivals** section). **Ninjutsu** is the fiendish and multi-faceted art of the *ninja*, the legendary spies and saboteurs of the feudal age. Though it was banned by the Tokugawa shogunate its techniques have been passed on in secret down to the present day.

Karate is a special case. Originating more than 1,500 years ago in China it was later introduced to the island of Okinawa, south of Kyushu, where it took on its modern characteristics. It arrived in Japan as recently as 1922 and has since become popular everywhere.

Among Western sports, baseball is undoubtedly the most popular and golf, in a country drastically short of space and entirely lacking in rolling hills, the most incongruous. Those high-netted enclosures you see on your trips around Tokyo are for practicing golf driving.

Soccer, rugby and American football are among other sports with plenty of amateur followers, while cricket has unaccountably failed to catch on. Japanese people often mistake it for croquet, the U.S. version of which, gateball is much enjoyed by old-age pensioners.

SPORTS : WHERE TO SEE AND DO

Sumo. Professional tournaments are held in Tokyo for 15 consecutive days in January, May and September at the New Kokugikan Sumo Hall in Ryogoku, Tokyo. Tel: (03) 623-5111.

Judo. Information is available the All-Japan Judo Federation (*Zen-ju-ren*). Tel: (03) 811-7151.

Aikido. Information from Tokyo Aikikai. Tel: (03) 203-9236.

The baroque mysteries of *sumo* are involved enough to sustain a lifetime's curiosity. LEFT AND ABOVE Scenes from the sumo wrestler's life. The wrestler at bottom left, opposite, is Chiyonofuji, a recent hero.

Karate. Information from World Union of Karate-do Organizations. Tel: (03) 503-6637/38.

For schedules of pro baseball and other sports see *Tour Companion* newspaper.

HOW DO THEY LIVE?

Meanwhile 121,000,000 human beings call Japan home. How do they make out? How do they live?

Take that youngish man in the blue

suit sitting opposite you in the subway, his face hidden behind a newspaper. How does he support himself? What sort of place does he live in? What does he believe? What are his dreams, his diversions?

FLOCKING OFF THE FARM

If we follow him off the train, he will lead us to his workplace: an office, the headquarters of a major company, 30 floors above Shinjuku in one of the skyscrapers there.

Thirty years ago white-collar jobs like his were an impossible dream for the majority. More than 50 per cent of the population were farmers or fishermen. By 1980 this proportion had dropped as low as 9.6 per cent. Meanwhile, since the oil shock, and

with the proliferation of mass-production methods (robots being the latest), the number of jobs in manufacturing has also begun to decline. In 30 years the *sarariman* (salaried worker) has replaced the farmer as Mr Average.

LIVING TO WORK

Arriving at 9 he'll work through to 5: that's the working day that gets into the statistics (the average worker put in 2,116 hours per year in 1984, about 116 more than his Western counterpart). However, he's likely to stay on for a couple of hours to finish up, then go off drinking with colleagues or clients. Japanese like to say they 'live to work' (in the West they do the opposite) and if it's not as true as it used to be there is still something in it. (It's the reason, incidentally, why traveling around Japan off season, between national holidays, can be a blissful experience: even if the weather is good almost everybody is at work.)

The government, believe it or not, has been trying to persuade the workforce to take it a little easier -- to stay home on Saturdays from time to time, for example. They are simply passing on the grumbles of other nations that the Japanese are too productive. The workforce does not like the idea -- or so they say, and many of them are sincere. Neither do many of their wives, some of whom are reportedly cracking up under the strain of having hubby around the house for two whole days.

Part of the reason for this is that the average Japanese home is not the best

ABOVE LEFT Golf is *de rigueur* for the ambitious executive. Lack of space in which to play it has brought into existence multi-storey driving ranges like this one in Tokyo.
RIGHT, TOP LEFT Modern gateposts, traditional roofs of a house in Beppu, Kyushu. RIGHT, BOTTOM showroom of Kei Tanimoto, a traditional potter in Iga, near Kyoto.

place in the world for relaxing. Let's follow our man home and have a look at it.

REGULATION RABBIT HUTCH

A few years ago an EEC report suggested that many Japanese houses resemble rabbit hutches. The remark stung, and stuck. They'll repeat it back to you, but it hurts. It's a bit too near the bone.

Our man is lucky enough to have his

own house. It has two stories, and underneath the Mediterranean blue tiles and the fancy mortar finish it has a traditional wooden post-and-beam structure (it was constructed from the top-down, starting with the roof). This structure means it sways in earthquakes (but does not collapse) and is cool in summer, but it's cold in winter and has a life expectancy of about 40 years.

It's a '4LDK' -- four rooms plus living-room, dining-kitchen, tiny bathroom and separate toilet, and it costs about US$150,000. Two of the rooms, one upstairs and one down, are tradi-

tional *tatami* rooms.

NATURE'S FRAGRANT CARPET

Tatami, rarely encountered outside Japan, is almost a sufficient reason for a visit to the country. The units are often called '*tatami* mats' which is confusing because 'mat' suggests a thin carpet. However, *tatami*, about two meters long and one meter wide (six feet by three feet), is nearly seven centimeters (three inches) thick, so it's better described as a pad or flooring block.

Tatami, found in almost every home in the country (though in modern homes there may be only one small *tatami* room), is made by neighborhood craftsmen and consists of many layers of tightly braided rice straw. The sleek surface, green when the pads are new, is closely woven matting made of a reed called *igusa*. The mat has an edging of cotton or silk.

At the threshold of a Japanese home one removes shoes and puts on slippers, but at the threshold of a *tatami* room one removes the slippers. The pad is solid but gives slightly under one's weight. It is soft enough to sleep on directly, (though this is rarely done) or for a baby to tumble around on. It is better than a carpet in summer as it remains cool, though in winter it can be downright chilly.

In wet weather or when the mat is new it gives off a sweet fragrance of straw. This sometimes makes foreigners feel nauseous but you grow accustomed to it quickly, and if you catch the smell again after an absence you may find it pulls at heartstrings you never knew existed. Then you'll know how it feels to be a Japanese coming home from abroad.

LEFT Decorative banner at a Shinto shrine.
RIGHT Elegant, elaborate, suffocatingly inhibited, the traditional Shinto wedding ceremony is typical of the ceremonial side of Japanese life.

Other Japanese smells which pull at heartstrings are:

the first mosquito coil of summer,

the smell of roasting tea (*hoji-cha* -- cheap and delicious), mothballs (dramatic changes in temperature between seasons mean that half one's wardrobe is moth-balled half the year) and

yuzu, a lime-like citron with a special fragrance, used in winter cooking.

All rooms in Japan are described according to the number of *tatami* mats which will fit flushly into them. It follows that rooms come in standard sizes: 3-mat, 4-1/2 mat, 6, 8, 10, 12 and so on. A 4-1/2 mat room is the classic size for a tea-ceremony (also for romantic assignations); 6 or 8 is normal for a living room. An 8-mat room is considered spacious, and when the only furnishings are a low table and a couple of flat cushions (*zabuton*) it feels spacious too, at least until you stand up. When crammed with a sofa, armchairs, a coffee table, a 60 cm. (24 in.) TV plus VTR, a stereo, bookcases, a cabinet full of unopened bottles of scotch and a personal computer, it no longer feels spacious at all.

This may be one reason our man puts in such long hours at the office.

WALL-TO-WALL PEOPLE

In our man's -- let's call him Saito -- in Mr Saito's house, however, it is the Western-style rooms which are full of furniture. The *tatami* room, the one upstairs, is full of people.

It's the bedroom, but only as long as the family is asleep. During the day it's a regular living room. At bedtime Mrs Saito pulls from the deep built-in closet *futon*, sheets, blankets, quilts (in winter) and pillows and spreads them on the *tatami*, one sleeping space per pad.

38

Futon are fluffy cotton mattresses, hung out in the sun every fine day. (Lazy bachelors don't hang out their *futon* and soon they become as hard as rice crackers, hence the phrase *'sembe-futon'*.)

All the Saitos sleep in this room, the younger of the two children between Mr and Mrs. This is one reason why love hotels are so popular in Japan, even with married couples. While Mr Saito collapses into bed, we can poke around the house. It's soon clear why he doesn't like to spend too much time here: it really *is* small. The garden, as he readily admits, is 'no bigger than a cat's forehead'.

LOVE AND MARRIAGE

In Japan, love and marriage increasingly go together like a horse and carriage. Mr and Mrs Saito met at work. He was a *sarariman* and she was an *o-eru* ('OL' = office lady). They dated in coffee shops, went to movies, admired sunsets and views of Mt. Fuji and occasionally went to love hotels where at first they only kissed.

More than 70 per cent of modern marriages are 'love marriages' like this, a dramatic increase over the number 20 years ago. The other 25-30 per cent are arranged.

The arranged marriage is very alien to Western thinking, but the Japanese point out its advantages. The *nakodo*, or go-between, who brings the couple together is a friend of both families who can see the economic, social, even emotional ramifications of the union for both sides without misty-eyed sentiment confusing the issue. Traditionally, marriage is thought of

ABOVE The band at a Shinto street festival in Osaka. BELOW The religious life: votive tablets, and strings of folded paper cranes, two ways of petitioning for good luck; and solitary worship at a temple in Nara.

39

not so much as a union of individuals as of families.

It's undeniable that this hard-headed system produces a lot of rock-solid marriages. Emotional expectations are realistically low and burgeoning friendship between the partners is a pleasant bonus.

It's also a humane system, at least these days, as both partners are given ample chance to meet, weigh each other up and, if it smells wrong, call the whole thing off. This happens frequently.

Living together for long periods without getting married is much, much rarer than in the West.

RITES OF PASSAGE

Like most Japanese couples, the Saitos solemnized their marriage with a Shinto ceremony at a wedding hall which has a shrine on the premises. (Shinto has shrines, *jinja*; Buddhism has temples, *o-tera*.) The groom wore a *moningu* (a morning suit) and the bride a silk wedding kimono of fantastically rich design and an elaborate bonnet to hide her 'horns of jealousy'. After the ceremony she changed into a Western wedding dress and veil and they cut a huge wedding cake. The whole performance, including costume and feast, consumed about 33 per cent of the year's income of the groom's family and about 50 per cent of the bride's. Not surprisingly, divorce is frowned upon. Although on the rise, it is about half as common as in Western Europe.

A Shinto shrine is the normal venue for a wedding, but when a member of the Saito family dies, a Buddhist priest will be called in. Hypocrisy? Confusion? The Japanese don't think so. Here's how it works.

HARMONY IN HEAVEN

Shinto is the native religion of Japan.

Like many other primitive religions, it is animistic: worship is directed at the phenomena of nature. The deities of Shinto are as varied and as multitudinous as the natural world itself, and basically anything which struck awe and wonder into the hearts of the early Japanese was exalted as a *kami* or deity: mountains, trees, waterfalls, foxes, infectious diseases, military heroes, emperors. The intellectual content of the religion was minimal. The idea of purification was central. *Kami-sama* were invoked to bring prosperity and ward off misfortune.

When tolerant Buddhism entered the country from the continent, it soon reached an accommodation with Shinto. The deities of Shinto became identified with Buddhist *Bodhisattvas*. Shrines and temples were often built on the same sacred ground. In the case of at least one sect, the Shugendo, the two religions fused.

Both religions have suffered different vicissitudes over the years, but essentially their demarcation lines are clear. Shinto, bright, pragmatic, recoiling from 'dirty' death, takes care of marriage; Buddhism, deeply philosophical, concerned with the essence of man's nature, takes care of death.

A THOUSAND GODS AND NONE

It is often said that the Japanese are no longer a religious people, but it is hard to say whether or not this is true. Certainly they are not secular in the way the people of the Protestant countries of Europe have become secular this century. Religious faith and ardor of the Christian type are rarities, but religious practices of all sorts are still extremely widespread.

When the people next door to the Saitos decided to rebuild their house, they went to stay with relatives nearby, but the grandmother of the house came to the site early each morning to pray to the *kami-sama* of the land to allow the operation to go through without harm. She put little cones of salt all round the site, with a lighted stick of incense in the center of each.

When the old building had been demolished, a square of young bamboo trees in leaf was erected, connected by sacred rope, and a Shinto priest called in to purify the ground. A similar ground-breaking ceremony took place at the site of a new TV factory nearby.

In addition to these and many other observances, street festivals being the most visible, a huge, bizarre panoply of new religions, usually focused on the teachings of a charismatic founder, has appeared in the last century.

Buddhism has been losing voltage for centuries. State-organized Shinto, associated with militarism, collapsed after the war. Less than one per cent of the population is Christian. Yet among ordinary people religious belief and practice persist, like a quiet background melody you can hear only if you listen hard.

THE CATFISH STIRS

It's still the middle of the night but suddenly and simultaneously Mr and Mrs Saito are awake: earthquake! The floor is moving underneath them and the wooden posts and beams are squeaking and groaning.

After a few seconds it stops. Neither of them has moved -- they quickly judged it was only a small quake -- but their pulses are racing all the same. There are three terrifying things, the Japanese used to say in the old days -- earthquakes, thunder and a father's anger. The latter two don't bother anybody much these days, but nobody gets used to earthquakes.

Japan suffers hundreds of them every year, and the Tokyo area is one

place where they are frequent. Most are too small to worry about, but every once in a while a big one strikes. Then, they say, the catfish which lives under Japan is thrashing its tail. The last really catastrophic one was the 1923 quake in which about 140,000 people died.

Fire is the worst hazard in an earthquake, so the first thing to do is to turn off the gas. Don't run outside but take cover, either under a table, in a doorway or in a small room such as the toi-

let (leave the door ajar or you may later have to crawl out the window). Dangers outside include falling roof tiles and collapsing stone or brick walls.

Wooden houses make a terrible noise but are resilient to all but the strongest quakes. Modern high-rise buildings in Tokyo are designed to ride out even those.

ABOVE Scene at a kindergarten in central Tokyo.

START RIGHT

After breakfast Mrs Saito packs her six-year-old boy off to school. She has high hopes for him. When he was three he was selected for a prestigious kindergarten not far away, and this might prove to have been the single most decisive event in his life. It put him in line for the top grade primary, junior high and high schools, and this in turn gives him a good chance of passing the entrance exam to one of the country's top universities -- maybe even Tokyo University (*Todai*), which is *the* top. Once that hurdle is behind him, a career in government or one of the top companies is practically assured.

A hundred years ago there was no word for 'competition' in Japanese. Now the education system is one of the most mercilessly competitive in the world. A high proportion of kids from age six upwards spend several hours a day after school at cramming schools (*juku*), memorizing the facts they need to give them an edge in the exams. 'Children without childhood', they were dubbed by one foreign observer.

At university they can relax and generally do. University students are renowned for doing as little as they can get away with. Who can blame them?

One reason for the harshness of Japan's education system is that the country's class structure, one of the world's most rigid a century ago, has almost collapsed in modern times. Nearly 80 per cent of the population believe themselves to be middle-class, while the level of literacy is an amazing 99 per cent. Japan is a true meritocracy -- which means the scramble to get to the top of the heap must be replayed remorselessly every generation.

COMPULSORY CRAMP

When the teacher enters, little Saito and all the other children stand and bow to him and the teacher bows back. Mrs Saito meets her *ikebana* (flower arrangement) teacher in the street and bows deeply, with her hands folded in front of her. Mr Saito does the same when he meets his boss in the morning, but with his hands at his side.

Japanese people start bowing when they are practically in the cradle. It's about as natural for them as yawning.

A bow is simply acknowledgement that there is a difference in status between the two parties. The greater the gap, the deeper the bow, which is why students bow more deeply than their teachers. Getting the angle exactly right is important. A year or two ago a department store installed a machine to help train staff how to bow correctly to customers.

Westerners usually look -- and feel -- weirdly obsequious when they attempt a Japanese bow. It is not expected: a nod and a smile will see you through.

VALE OF TEARS

When Mr Saito finally puts down his paper, try giving him a nod and a smile. He needs all the encouragement he can get. Every morning he has to struggle in to the centre of the city on a transportation system which is one of the most crowded, as well as one of the most efficient, in the world: some 4,000,000 commuters,

plus 3,500,000 other passengers, ride Tokyo's Japan National Railways trains every day.

This prospect stretches ahead of him five or six days a week, for the rest of his working life -- or at least until the regular retiring age of 60. Mr Saito's company, which is one of the larger and more prestigious, offers him and most other male employees lifetime employment. It's a great prospect when things are going well, but when he's wedged under someone's armpit in the morning crush he can't be blamed for his dreams of fleeing somewhere and opening a coffee shop or *pension*-style guesthouse.

Mrs Saito's life is not a bed of roses either. She is one of the 31 per cent of Japanese women who graduated from a university -- just a two-year one, admittedly -- but it landed her nothing better than a clerical job in the company and no prospects of advancement.

When she married she submitted to expectations and resigned. Like many educated women she's in a rut, with nothing to do with her wits but take care of an ultra-convenient home and prod her children on to ever-greater educational achievement. The *fyoiku mama* -- 'education-obsessed mom' -- is a phenomenon of the new Japan.

So both Mr and Mrs Saito have their frustrations. The easiest way to forget them is to take a trip to the neighborhood *pachinko* parlor.

Pachinko is the vertical pinball game which began in Japan after the war and spread like fire. At the latest count, there were some 9,617 *pachinko* parlors nationwide. In a dense metallic cacophony of cascading silver balls, electronic slurrings and slushings and taped martial music, the troubled soul can fix

ABOVE LEFT For some, computer classes start young. This little girl is pre-school. ABOVE The people-pushers on Japan's railways wear white gloves.

his eyes on the machine and drift away. Continual refinements ensure that he doesn't get tired of it: some of the recent machines have tiny TV sets embedded in the center.

There are prizes to be won -- they can be exchanged for cash illegally, at nearby shops -- but except for the very keen or the very poor they are not the main incentive. Escape from reality is the name of the game.

ABOVE AND LEFT *Pachinko* parlors, where the jaded citizen can be alone in the crowd. Their owners are among the nation's biggest tax evaders.

Despite all the hard work, puritanism is a philosophy which has never taken root in Japan. The Japanese are a pleasure-loving people, and the good news is that a surprising number of their unique diversions are perfectly accessible to visitors, the enjoyment almost unaffected by the language barrier.

Love of pleasure is engraved in the national character. While the Christian Bible virtually opens with a story of sin and expulsion, the Japanese national myth revolves around a rude dance.

Affronted by another of the gods, the sun goddess (ancestress, it was believed, of the imperial family) shut herself away in a cave, plunging the world into darkness. The other deities gathered round the mouth of the cave and one of them performed a hilariously indecent dance, causing the others to fall about laughing. The sun goddess within was overcome with curiosity. She emerged, and has been shining ever since.

THEATER

Noh

The medieval *noh* theater, which nearly gave out at the start of the modern period, is strong and active again now and has had a big influence on the avant-garde theater of the West. This highly formalized and unrealistic type of drama was the favorite of one of the early shoguns, who had parts specially written for him and liked to rehearse before going into battle.

The beauty of *noh* is in the hypnotic and mysterious dancing, the masks -- some blander than the Mona Lisa, some frighteningly demonic -- and in the uncannily timeless atmosphere induced by these and by the music of drums and flute, punctuated by low wails and whoops. In this unworldly setting, where rules of time and space seem to be in suspension, old tales of loyalty, jealous passion and reincarnation unfold.

It is this atmosphere and the techniques used to bring it about which have excited the most interest in *noh* in modern times, but the stories too have an uncanny power. The great writer Yukio Mishima, notorious for his death by *seppuku* (hara-kiri) in 1970,

reworked a selection of them into Western-style one-act plays and reading these is perhaps the easiest way to get a feeling for the quality of *noh*. They have been published in English as *Five Modern Noh Plays*.

Noh is slow by the standards of modern theater and feels very ancient indeed -- much more so than *kabuki*, for example -- but once you are wrapped up in it you will forget about time. Try it, if only for the deep, meditative calm it can induce.

The **Kanze Noh-gakudo** (Shibuya, tel: (03) 469-5241) and the **Hosho Noh-gakudo** (Suidobashi, tel: (03) 811-4843) are two excellent places to see *Noh*. Prices: ¥3,000 and ¥2,500-¥5,000 respectively. Performances start at 5.30 or 6 p.m. Check *Tour Companion* newspaper, available in hotels, Tourist Information Centers, etc. for details.

Kabuki

Kabuki comes from the verb *kabuku*

which means to flirt, to frolic. It was first applied to another rude dance performed by a legendary lady called O-Kuni on a dry river bed in Kyoto.

This remarkable thespian, said to have been rather plain but exceptionally clever, laid the foundations of the new art form at exactly the same time that Shakespeare was laying the foundations of his.

To add substance and interest to her dances she borrowed boldly from the

noh theater and other contemporary forms, infusing her performances with the vigor and coarse spontaneity which had been deliberately drained from the aristocratic *noh*. Her performances finished with a 'general dance' in which the spectators were welcome to take part -- in any way they liked.

We can be sure that they did not restrain themselves, for the all-woman group was shortly closed down by the shogun on grounds of immorality.

It was replaced by an overtly homosexual all-male company from which *kabuki* as it exists today developed. Throughout the long peace of the Tokugawa period, *kabuki* was the mouthpiece as well as the chief delight of the Edo townsman -- merchant, shopkeeper, artisan. His materialism, his dash, his sentimentality and superstitiousness all found voice in the plays. As nothing much has changed in the productions of *kabuki* in a century or more, it offers the best insight into the tastes of that gaudy period -- as well as being thoroughly enjoyable in its own right.

Everything in *kabuki* is on a huge scale. The stage, wide and low, is equipped with traps, revolves and has every mechanical trick known to pantomime, carried off with a dozen times more panache and conviction. Costumes are gorgeous in the extreme -- some weigh in at 18 kg. (40 lb.) -- and the *hanamichi* or 'flower walk' which runs from the stage to the back of the auditorium allows punters in the stalls to see them close up.

The plays go on all day, starting at 11.30 a.m. The longeurs of the slow scenes are long indeed, but theaters like the **Kabuki-za** in Ginza are crammed with restaurants and kiosks to which

---

ABOVE Performance of a *Noh* play at Meiji Shrine in Tokyo.

the bored or hungry can retreat at any time.

Kabuki is a theater of spectacle and deserves to be seen close up. Then the full impact of the show -- the dances, the transformations, the unearthly music of *shamisen*, flutes, clappers and drums coming from both sides of the stage, as well as the pathos of the separations and suicides and the glamour of the great battles -- and all the vanity and charm of the Edo period pour over the happy spectator in a huge wave.

The Kabuki-za is perhaps the best place to see *kabuki*, although the **Shimbashi Embujo** and the **National Theater** are also fine. Tickets for *kabuki* and all other plays in Tokyo may be purchased from **Playguides** ticketing agencies, located in many department stores around town. Prices are lower than at the box office. Start queueing at 10 a.m. outside Kabuki-za to see that day's performance. Prices: between ¥1,500 and ¥10,000 Kabuki-za, tel: (03) 541-3131; between ¥1,000 and ¥3,000 (National Theater tel: (03) 265-7411.

Bunraku

Bunraku, the puppet theater, started life at the same time as *kabuki*, shares many of its characteristics and was long in competition with it. It is certainly the most elaborate puppet drama in the world, and perhaps the only one which goes beyond the broadly comic to take on pathos and tragedy. Considering its age and strangeness, it is surprisingly easy to enjoy.

The largest of the puppets are two-thirds human size and require three operators, the master taking the head and right hand and his assistants the left hand and the feet. The repertoire, much of which it shares with *kabuki*, includes tales of revenge, sacrifice and suicide.

The love suicide plays are among the most engaging. Many of them written about true episodes of thwarted love between humble shopkeepers and geisha which were currently in the news, they abound with realistic detail and are sometimes really moving. Many a hard-bitten Westerner has found himself mopping the tears from his face at the climax of such a play.

Good seats are vital for the enjoyment of *bunraku*, even more so than for *kabuki*, due to the size of the puppets. Master puppet operators work with their faces uncovered but when the play has you in its grip you will find you have forgotten about them. If you get tired of looking at the puppets, shift your attention slightly to the right and admire the art of the *joruri*, narrators who, augmented by a *shamisen* player, recite the play's story and take on all the parts.

Bunraku is staged in May, September and December of each year at Tokyo's pleasant but aseptic **National Theater**. A trip to the **Asahi-za Theater** in Osaka, where the company is based, would allow one to savor the *bunraku* atmosphere to the full.

Contemporary Theater

Modern theater flourishes in Tokyo, too. At theaters such as the **Nissei Gekijo** and the **Teikoku Geki** the *kabuki* tradition manifests itself in the elaborate staging and the tendency to glittering fantasy in modern works, some of which feature stars borrowed from the *kabuki* companies. Internationally known companies such as the Waseda Shogekijo and Tenjo Sajiki, playwrights like Hisashi Inoue and Juro Kara, theaters like the **Honda Gekijo** in Shimo-kitazawa -- all these demonstrate the liveliness of Japanese contemporary theater. See the monthly *To-*

RIGHT Carp streamers, hoisted in preparation for the Boy's Festival on 5 May. Carp are admired for the way they fight their way upstream, overcoming all obstacles. Growing boys are exhorted to do likewise.

kyo Journal for details of these and more.

Another theater experience for the curious is **Takarasuka**, a modern all-female company which stages lavish and sticky-sweet fantasies in Tokyo every six or eight weeks.

FESTIVALS

Christmas is the time when most foreigners in Japan tend to get homesick. The festival is only observed by the tiny minority of Christians and by the department stores. The Japanese calen-

dar is spotted with so many festivals full of resonance and seasonal cheer that one more is not really necessary.

For a start, there is **O-shogatsu**, the New Year holiday when nearly all shops and offices close for several days and Japanese people swarm by the million to popular shrines such as Meiji in Tokyo to pray for a good year. Special food is eaten -- all prepared, in theory, before 1 January so that Mum can take a rest, too -- kites are flown and an ancient form of battledore and shuttlecock is enjoyed. Around midnight on New Year's Eve the bells of Buddhist temples boom out 108 times across cities, towns and villages and people everywhere gulp bowls of *soba* (buckwheat noodles). All these are ways of getting off to a good start.

The day for spotting the gaudiest ki-

monos is 15 January, when girls and boys who have reached the age of 20 during the previous 365 days celebrate the event with shrine-visiting and parties. This is **Seijin-no-hi** or Coming-of-Age Day.

Boys and girls both have their special days, girls on 3 March -- **Hina matsuri** -- and boys on 5 May, a festival called **Tango-no-sekku**. In both cases traditional dolls are dusted off and admired. You know the boy's festival is coming up by the huge, brightly colored windsock carp flying from high poles in many gardens. Boys are exhorted to be as brave as the carp, which fights its way upstream.

The spring and autumn equinoxes, *higan*, have a significance they have long lost in the West. At these times the sun sets dead west, which is the location of the heavenly Pure Land according to one school of Buddhism, so at *higan* graves are visited and prayers offered for the repose of the dead.

The biggest festival in honor of ancestors, however, occurs in August and is called **O-bon**. This is the year's second major holiday, after *O-shogatsu*, and many millions of Japanese with roots in the countryside go back home at this time. The spirits of the dead are welcomed back into the home, the family taking lanterns to the graveyard to light their way. As part of the general party, made gay by the *bon-odori* dancing, small portions of the dead ones' preferred foods are set aside for them, and on the last night of the holiday paper lantern boats are set afloat on local streams and rivers to light the spirits' way back to the celestial world.

Beauties of the season are admired at fitting times -- cherry blossoms in

LEFT Inauspicious *o-mikuji*, fortune-telling papers, tied to bushes at Heian Shrine in Kyoto. RIGHT, ABOVE Some girls still dress up in their finery for New Year's holiday.
RIGHT, BELOW Tokyo's firemen dress up for New Year's too, and demonstrate traditional acrobatics.

51

April, the moon in September. Both are occasions of more carousing than poetry.

Another good occasion for kimono-viewing is the **Shichi-go-san** (Seven-five-three) festival on 15 November. On this day girls of seven, boys of five and three-year-olds of either sex are dressed up in finery -- at frightening expense -- and taken to visit local shrines.

Finally two festivals which are not marked on the calendar, and are generally celebrated by a trip to the bank, occur in June and December: the days when a *sarariman* receives his twice-yearly bonus. This may amount to as much as six times his monthly salary, so it's certainly something to celebrate.

The lifestyle of the average Japanese may seem rather bleak in Western terms: cramped living conditions, few holidays, a dogged dedication to work. But the wealth of annual festivals, each with its special atmosphere and its special treats, does a lot to even the balance.

Then there are street festivals (*matsuri*). Large and small, magnificent and humble, these erupt across Japan at all times of the year.

Sometimes it is the simplest festivals which are the most memorable. Take the ubiquitous neighborhood festivals, for example.

It is the local shrine which, all over Japan, is the focus of such festivals. There, locked away behind heavy doors, are the *o-mikoshi*, the miniature portable shrines in which the shrine's deity is said to reside for the duration of its day out.

Supervised by an aged priest, the young blades of the area, looking their most macho in sweat bands, *happi* coats and straw sandals, heave the

ABOVE LEFT Costumed warriors at Nikko Grand Festival, ABOVE RIGHT a young participant in Kyoto's Aoi Matsuri (Hollyhock Festival) and BELOW kite and tattooed kite-flyer at Hamamatsu's festival.

weighty shrine aloft on poles and begin their long, gay and grueling parade around the neighborhood. The often mean and tatty streets are transformed by it. Watch as one approaches. On the shoulders of one of the men preceding the shrine is a little girl whose elfin face has been whitened with powder, her lips painted crimson, red dots put in the corners of her eyes, mauve shadow spread on her lids and a livid white gash marked down the bridge of her nose -- she looks supernatural. She carries a baton in either hand and waves them extravagantly, conducting the movements of the *o-mikoshi* in perfect time.

And here it comes -- the shrine itself. The way it lurches from one side of the street to the other, comes to a dead halt, leaps suddenly forward, while all the time bobbing up and down in time with the bearers' hoarse cries -- *'Wasshoi! Wasshoi!'* -- it seems to be imbued with life. The big golden phoenix on the summit sparkles as it rears from side to side, the bells on the roof jangle. The bearers, 20 or more of them, heave and strain, sweating freely, all the time keeping up a comic pigeon-toed, knee-jerking dance that goes on all day. Two men stay by the hinged handles on both sides of the shrine, banging them down in time with the cries, and at the back, hanging on for dear life to the two twisted cotton ties which are attached to the ends of the bearers' poles, are the two helmsmen who keep it on course.

In a few minutes it's gone, but if you wait an hour or two it will be back. The parade goes on all day, rain or shine, spectators or no spectators, till the bearers are dazed with exhaustion and they have tied their town in knots like a cat with a ball of wool, reaffirming the

OVERLEAF One of the massive kites flown competitively at Hamamatsu's festival.

53

solidarity and strength of their community. That's what the festival is really about.

Every visitor to Japan should try to experience at least one festival, both for the sake of your camera and to get some inkling of the ancient ties of effort and brotherhood which keep Japanese communities together. Below are listed some of the most famous and splendid.

TOKYO

Dezome-shiki or New Year Ceremony (6 January). Firemen's parade, featuring a display of traditional acrobatics

by firemen on top of tall bamboo ladders. Location: Chuo-dori, Harumi (Tsukiji station, subway).

Zojoji Matsuri (13-15 April). Large and colorful procession in memory of St. Honen, founder of the Jodo sect of Buddhism; continues for three days. Location: Zojoji Temple, Shiba Park (Shibakoen station, Toei Mita municipal subway.)

Kanda Myojin Matsuri (Mid-May). One of the capital's two greatest *matsuri* (the other one is at Hie Shrine) and one of the 'big three' nationwide, this festival involves many magnificent *o-mikoshi* and ancient dances. Location:

Kanda Myojin Shrine, Tokyo (Kanda station, JNR). Held on even-numbered years -- 86, 88, 90...

Sanja Matsuri (Mid-May). A famous and splendid festival, featuring more than 50 huge *o-mikoshi* and troops of Shinto priests. Location: Asakusa Shrine (Asakusa station, subway).

Sanno Matsuri (Mid-June). The other of Tokyo's two great *matsuri* with dancers, wood-wheeled carts, *o-mikoshi* and gilded lions' heads. Location: Hie Shrine, Tokyo. Held on odd-numbered years -- 87, 89, 91...

Hanabi Taikai or Grand Fireworks Display (end July/beginning August). Fireworks are a spectacular feature of Japan's sticky summer, and this recently revived display is one of the best in the country. Time: 7.15-8.15 p.m. Arrive early. Location: Sumida River at Asakusa (Asakusa station, subway).

NIKKO

Grand Festival of Toshogu Shrine (17-18 May). A grand procession recreates the days of the Tokugawa shogunate against the background of Japan's most gorgeous shrine. Location: Toshogu Shrine, Nikko, Tochigi Prefecture.

KAMAKURA

Tsurugaoka Hachimangu Spring Festival (2nd to 3rd Sunday in April). Many parades and other events under the cherry blossoms in Japan's medieval capital, just an hour from Tokyo. Location: Tsurugaoka Hachiman Shrine, Kamakura, Kanagawa Prefecture.

Hachiman Matsuri (Mid-September). A festival featuring *yabusame*, the martial art of archery on horseback, in the grounds of Kamakura's biggest shrine. Location as above.

HAKONE

Hakone Daimyo Gyoretsu or Hakone Feudal Lord Procession (3 November). About 200 local people in feudal costumes parade through the streets of the handsome old spa town of Hakone-Yumoto. Location: Sounji Temple, Hakone-Yumoto, Kanagawa Prefecture.

SHIMODA

Kurofune Matsuri or Black Ships Festival (mid-May). The arrival of the American Commodore Perry in his 'black ships' was the most crucial single event in the opening of Japan to the outside world. The event is recreated and commemorated at this port in the Izu Peninsula, 2-1/2 hours by rail from Tokyo. Location: Gyokunseji Temple, Shimoda, Shizuoka Prefecture.

HAMAMATSU

Hamamatsu Odakoage or Big Kite Flying (3-5 May). One of Japan's most famous kite festivals in which kites of all sizes engage in battles. The expert contestants try to cut the strings of opposing kites by means of glass or other sharp objects fastened to their own strings. Hamamatsu is a town famous for musical instruments and motorcycles and is nearly two hours by Shinkansen ('bullet' train) from Tokyo. Location: sand dunes some three miles from town. Shuttle buses leave from outside the station on festival days.

KYOTO

Aoi Matsuri or Hollyhock Festival (15 May). Japan's oldest festival, dating from the sixth century, and one of the most elegant. The procession features an imperial messenger and his retinue in costumes from the Heian period and a cart with huge wooden wheels decorated with wisteria flowers and drawn by a garlanded ox led by ropes of orange silk. Location: Kamigamo and Shimogamo Shrines, Kyoto.

Mifune Matsuri (3rd Sunday in May). Prettily decorated boats with the figureheads in the shape of dragons and phoenixes sail down the river Oi, bearing musicians, commemorate the river-bourne excursions of the Heian court. Location: River Oi at Arashiyama, ner Kyoto.

Gion Matsuri (17-24 July). Perhaps the single most famous festival in Japan and another of the 'big three'. The procession features towering, teetering carts which are dragged through the streets, all of ancient origin and each with a story to tell. Many other events

connected with the festival occur throughout July. Location: Yasaka Shrine, Higashiyama-ku, and Shijo-Kawaramachi amusement quarter, Kyoto.

Daimonji Okuribi or Great Bonfire Event (16 August). A great bonfire on a Kyoto hillside burns in the shape of the character *Dai* (大), meaning 'Great', and is visible for miles. Location: Mt. Nyoigadake, Kyoto.

Jidai Matsuri or Festival of the Ages (22 October). For a vivid rundown on how the costumes of Japan's ruling

LEFT AND ABOVE Two more scenes from Hamamatsu's kite festival.

NARA

Mando-e or Lantern-Lighting Ceremony (3 or 4 February). All 3,000 lanterns of Kasuga Shrine are lit, welcoming the coming of spring. The ceremony is repeated on 15 August in the *o-bon* season (Festival of the Dead) to light the way for visits from de-

class have changed over the last millennium this festival is unbeatable. The long procession begins with soldiers of the Meiji period (1868-1912) and works backwards to the nobles and archers of the eighth century. The attention to authenticity of detail is meticulous. Location: Heian Shrine, Kyoto.

Ukai or Cormorant Fishing (11 May-15 October). A lighted stick draws *ayu*, a type of trout, to the surface of the river where cormorants on leashes are waiting to snap them up and deliver them whole to the waiting boatmen. A highly popular occasion for a summer party on the water. Location: Nagara River, Gifu Prefecture, and Uji River, Kyoto Prefecture.

THIS PAGE AND OPPOSITE, LEFT Scenes from Kyoto's *Aoi Matsuri* (Hollyhock Festival). Many of the costumes and hairstyles date from the Heian Period (794-1185). The great mound of flowers OPPOSITE, LEFT sits on top of an ancient parasol. OPPOSITE PAGE, RIGHT Decorative prow of a boat in the *Mifune Matsuri* (Boat Festival), another of Kyoto's spring events.

parted spirits. Location: Kasuga Shrine, Nara.

Onio-shiki or Demon-Driving Ceremony (4 February, but variable). 1 February marks the end of winter and the beginning of spring and is the season of *setsubun* when the chant of 'Demons out! Luck in!' is heard, and roasted beans are chucked around the house and elsewhere as a means of ritual purification. This rite is taken to a picturesquely literal extreme at Kofukuji Temple, where men dressed as demons invade the temple grounds and are then chased out by disguised priests. Location: Kofukuji Temple, Nara. (Also at Horyuji Temple, Nara, and Nagata Shrine, Kobe.)

O-mizutori Matsuri or Water-Drawing Festival (12 March). A solemn evening festival, the greatest event of the year, at the temple which houses Nara's Great Buddha. Huge torches illuminate the temple, the eerie wailing of conchs echoes through the air and at midnight the festival culminates in the drawing of holy water from the Wakasa well. Location: Todaiji Temple, Nara.

OSAKA
Tenjin Matsuri (24-25 July). A richly picturesque festival with processions on both land and river, this is the third

of the 'big three'. A Chinese-style lion dance and a huge drum played by six men in immensely tall hats are among the attractions. Location: Temmangu Shrine, Osaka.

HIMEJI
Kenka Matsuri or Fighting Festival (14-15 October). One of the few festivals in Japan with an element of danger. Participating *o-mikoshi*-bearing teams jostle and barge one another in an effort to come first. Location: Matsubara Hachiman Shrine, Himeji City, Hyogo Prefecture.

HIROSHIMA
Heiwa Matsuri or Peace Festival (6 August). Hiroshima's most important annual event, commemorating those who died as a result of the atom bomb which fell on the city at 8.15 a.m. on 6 August 1945. A solemn occasion with songs of peace, prayers and lighted paper lanterns floated down the river. Location: Heiwa Koen (Peace Park), Hiroshima.

MIYAJIMA
Kangen-sai Matsuri or Music Festival (late July or early August). A fleet of brightly decorated boats makes a sea parade in the vicinity of the holy island of Miyajima, accompanied by *gagaku*, the ancient music of the imperial court. Location: Itsukushima Shrine,

Miyajima, Hiroshima Prefecture.

SHIKOKU

Awa Odori or Awa Dance (15-18 August). Mid-August is the season of *o-bon*, the Festival of the Dead, much more cheerful than it sounds as it is the occasion for the spirits of dead loved ones to return home for a season, and they are given a properly uproarious welcome. Dancing and festivities take place nationwide, but Tokushima in Shikoku is famous for making a really big thing of it; in fact, this may be Japan's most truly festive festival. Parading, dancing and drinking continue day and night throughout the three-day period. Location: Tokushima City, Tokushima Prefecture, Shikoku.

NAGASAKI

Peiron or Boat Race (early June). Thirty-five men crowd into each of a number of long and bulky boats and paddle to the rhythm of gongs and drums as they strive to win this grueling, Chinese-derived race. Location: Nagasaki City, Nagasaki Prefecture, Kyushu.

Okunchi Matsuri (7-9 October). Nagasaki is one of the closest spots in Japan to China, and the fabulously gaudy carts and dragons in this brilliant festival show strong Chinese influence. Location: Suwa Shrine, Nagasaki.

TAKAYAMA

Sanno Matsuri (14-15 April) and **Takayama Matsuri** (9-10 October). Takayama has 23 enormous and enormously ornate *yatai* or festival wagons, covered in carvings and tapestries, some with mechanical figures which perform tricks. Twelve of these are

---

dragged through the streets in the spring Sanno Festival, the other 11 in the autumn Yahata festival: both are among the nation's most magnificent. The 23 beautiful old floats in these processions testify to the strength of tradition in this well-preserved town, located on the old 'back way' from Edo (Tokyo) to Kyoto. Location: Hie Shrine, Takayama, Gifu Prefecture.

KANAZAWA

Hyakuman-goku-sai or The Lord's Million-Measures-of-Rice Event (13-15 June). A large and fascinatingly varied parade, including geisha old-fashioned firemen, and demonstrations of the tea ceremony. Location: Oyama Shrine, Kanazawa, Ishikawa Prefecture.

SENDAI

Tanabata Matsuri or Seventh of July Festival (old calendar) (6-8 August). Two stars, Kengyu and Shokujo, are separated by the Milky Way, but once a year around this time they meet. The annual rendezvous of the heavenly lovers, as a Chinese fairy tale describes them, is celebrated with a gaudy but processionless festival in many parts of the country. Sendai's is the most famous. The streets are hung with extremely elaborate decorations, originally made of paper, now often, and regrettably, of polythene. Location: Sendai, Miyagi Prefecture.

MATSUSHIMA

Matsushima Toronagashi or Lantern Event (16 August). In the island-spotted waters of this famous bay, thousands of little boat lanterns are set sailing. Location: Matsushima, Miyagi Prefecture.

AOMORI

Nebuta Matsuri or Dummy Festival (1-7 August). Two million people pour into this otherwise undistinguished city in the far north of Honshu for one of the most dramatic of summer festivals. The special feature is the procession of huge, beautifully painted and illuminated papier mâché floats which are hauled drunkenly through the city during the festival's two-day climax. Location: Aomori City.

AKITA

Kanto Matsuri or Balancing Festival (5-7 August). Reputedly the most enjoyable of Tohoku's 'Big Three' summer festivals (the other two are in Sendai and Aomori), this festival features the boys and men of the city balancing huge bamboo frameworks covered with lanterns and weighing 60-odd Kilos on their foreheads, shoulders, hips, hands and even mouths while they slink down the street to the accompaniment of traditional music. Location: Akita City.

SAPPORO

Yuki Matsuri or Snow Festival (Wednesday to Saturday of first week in February). The capital of the northernmost large island, Hokkaido, takes advantage of its freezing winter with a famously kitschy festival of snow sculpture, plus a costumed parade and skating. Shrewd publicity has induced foreigners to visit the festival in large numbers, but some have complained recently that it is basically a PR stunt for the Self-Defense Forces who construct many of the larger sculptures, and that it lacks the spontaneity and fun of more traditional festivals. Location: Sapporo, Hokkaido.

The festivals listed above are not only fascinating and charming in their own right, but most of them occur in towns and cities which offer other compelling reasons for a visit These places crop up again in the two chapter

The lady of the house welcomes guests to her mellow, elegant, 100-year-old *ryokan* in Narai.

that follow, **Japan: The Broad Highway** and **Off the Beaten Track**, where their particular attractions are described more fully. By careful planning it is possible for the visitor to enjoy both a famous festival and the more serene pleasures of sightseeing in one and the same trip.

Besides these regular, annual events there are many once-only festivals around the country every year, and innumerable tiny but delightful neighborhood festivals of the type described at the beginning of this section. Details of the former can be obtained from the Tourist Information Centers (TIC) in Tokyo and Kyoto; stumbling across the latter is a matter of luck.

Checking with the TIC is a must anyway, whatever the festival: dates vary from year to year, old festivals give up the ghost, even older ones are suddenly revived. A photostat 'Calendar of Events' is issued by the TIC for each month, and this contains dates and useful details. If you can't get to one of

ABOVE AND OPPOSITE The *onsen* (hot spring) phenomenon. ABOVE AND OPPOSITE, TOP Beppu's massive jungle bath, located inside a building resembling an aircraft hangar. OPPOSITE, BELOW LEFT Steam spews from the ground in one of Beppu's sulphurous 'hells'. OPPOSITE, BELOW RIGHT A lady enjoying Ibusuki's hot sand baths.

their offices, use the new Japan Travel Phone service, toll-free outside Tokyo and Kyoto, to get information. For details of this service see **Travelers' Tips**.

RYOKAN

The single most pleasant way to immerse yourself in things Japanese is to stay at a *ryokan* or Japanese inn. Hotels all over the world are much the same and, like airports, have the effect of homogenizing the experience of travel. In a *ryokan*, on the other hand, the Japanese experience is at its most piquant. Furthermore, if you are prepared to put up with some inconveniences, you will probably end up agreeing that a good *ryokan* is at least the equal of a good hotel for comfort.

But make sure it is a real *ryokan*. The building will usually be no higher than two storeys and constructed of wood, and there should be a garden, however small. In contrast to much else in Japan's modern cities its appearance, with pine trees, paper windows and a step up from the *genkan* (entrance) to the body of the house, should declare plainly that you are now in Japan.

A maid or the mistress will greet you at the entrance with a polite bow. Leave your shoes there, put on slippers and follow her to your room.

If the *ryokan* is very traditional, the door to your room will be a sliding one made of paper and flimsy wood, and there will be no lock. There is no need to worry about the safety of your belongings -- the honesty of the Japanese is one of the most relaxing things about their country -- but, if you worry all the same, leave valuables with the maid. Nowadays some *ryokan* rooms are equipped with safes.

The floor of the room will be covered with blocks of *tatami* flooring (see **How Do They Live?** for a description), so leave your slippers outside. In the

room's *tokonoma* (alcove) will be displayed a painting or a piece of calligraphy and an arrangement of freshly cut flowers. There will be a low table in the room with *zabuton* (seating pads) around it; in winter the table will be replaced with a *kotatsu*, a table with an electric heat-ring element underneath, covered with a quilt under which guests toast their feet. You will sit at the table to drink tea and later to eat the evening meal, except in some larger *ryokan* which have separate dining rooms.

Ryokan food is Japanese food and is often very good. You may be offered Western food but would be wise to reject this firmly: say *'Washoku kudasai'* -- 'Japanese food, please.'

Before supper you will generally be invited to take a bath. This is often a large one used by all the guests, and if your *ryokan* is in a hot spring area this may be the high point of your stay. For correct bathing procedure see **Baths**, below. You will be provided with a *yukata* (a light sleeping kimono) to wear after the bath.

After supper the maid will clear away the table and spread out the *futon* (mattress), quilt and pillow which are stored in the room's closet. The pillow may be filled with rice husks and rather harder than what you are used to. It will, however, help to keep your head cool. Cool head, warm feet: that's the healthy way, the Japanese believe.

In the morning the bed-making procedure will be reversed and you will eat breakfast in your room. Two meals are generally included in the *ryokan*'s tariff. Check-out is by 10 or 11 a.m.

Most visitors fall in love with the *ryokan* experience, but there are undeniable drawbacks. Sitting on the floor becomes painful before long. Toilets are of the crouching variety. There are no Western-sized desks to write or read at.

The ideal answer would be a hybrid, combining the best of the traditional elements -- the wooden structure, the *tatami*, the *futon*, the bath -- with Western conveniences. Unfortunately, no *ryokan* fitting this description exists as yet -- or so we believe. Any reader who discovers one would do us a favor by letting us know.

Tax and service charges, as well as two meals, are usually included in the price quoted. This may be as low as ¥6,000 (or even ¥4,000, though don't expect much luxury for that price) or it may be a great deal higher. Kyoto's famous **Sumiya Ryokan** costs between ¥35,000 and ¥40,000 per night, which makes it nearly twice as expensive as the swankiest hotel in Tokyo. Reservations at a *ryokan* can be made through a travel agent.

BATHS

Water is the one natural resource with which Japan is blessed in really ample quantities. And due to the countrywide volcanic activity, hot water, rich in health-giving salts and minerals, putters and bubbles out of the earth in innumerable places and has long provided the Japanese with one of their cheapest, yet richest, delights: hot spring bathing.

Soak away the day's strains in the startlingly hot water of the large bath in your *ryokan* and you are already tasting that pleasure. But to get the full effect you should travel to one of the many resort towns which have grown up around particularly generous or salubrious hot springs. The water may be murky and reek of sulfur but once you are immersed in it you will feel the difference.

Fantastic medicinal properties are claimed for many baths and almost all are said to be good for 'ladies' sicknesses' and skin diseases. The beautifully preserved skin of some of the old ladies who live in hot spring areas suggests that the latter claim at least is true. But for most visitors, Japanese as well as foreign, the real reason for bathing is that it is one of the idlest and easiest of pleasures.

Several renowned bathing areas are described in the chapters that follow. Among the most famous and/or accessible are:

Hakone-Yumoto. 1-1/2 hours by Odakyu lines Romance Car, a truly luxurious train, from Shinjuku in Tokyo, this is a charming old spa town on the old Tokaido road to Kyoto.

Atami. 'Shinjuku-on-sea', 55 minutes by Shinkansen ('bullet' train) from Tokyo, Atami is one of the biggest spa resorts in Japan and the best place to see metropolitan Japanese at play. Too much concrete for some nature lovers. Be sure to take the Shinkansen's Kodama train: the Hikari flashes straight through Atami.

Beppu and **Ibusuki.** These are two of the most famous spas in Kyushu, the southernmost of Japan's main islands. Both feature hot sand baths, in which the lucky guest is buried to the waist or beyond in naturally steaming hot sand, and jungle baths, huge tropical greenhouses dotted with pools of different colors and temperatures.

Noboribetsu Spa. One of the baths in this town in the northernmost island of Hokkaido is one of the few attested mixed baths still remaining in Japan.

Bath Etiquette

It will assure anxious natives that you know what you are about if you follow the same procedure as you do when bathing in your *ryokan*. Before entering the bath, wash yourself with soap and hot water and rinse off thoroughly, sitting on one of the small stools provided and using hot and cold water from the taps. Rinse the small towel or flannel you have brought with you and take it

with you into the bath to preserve your modesty. You may like to follow Japanese custom and place it on your head while you are in the water.

Don't let your hair get in the water. If the bath is mixed refrain from obvious staring or drooling. Rinse again on leaving the bath, in cold water if you like, but avoid pouring a bucketful over your neighbor.

The average cost of staying overnight at a spa (*onsen* in Japanese) is ¥12,000 including dinner and breakfast. Reservations, particularly at weekends

and holiday seasons, are essential. Solicit help from the TIC.

Warning! The Japanese bath is *hot* -- temperatures range from 35° to 60°C (95° to 140°F) plus. The hardest part is getting in. Once in, if you then sit still, your troubles are over (until you have

ABOVE Stark, fluid, the Chinese character for fan -- *'ogi'* -- the *noren* half-curtain of this restaurant in central Tokyo.

to get out). However, for older people, especially people suffering from high blood pressure, the temperatures can be dangerous. If you want to risk it anyway, turn on the cold tap before entering and stay in that cooler region.

For people who have no time or inclination to make a special trip to a resort, and who are staying in, say, a Western-style business hotel and who have no time or inclination to make a special trip to a resort, a way to sample the pleasures of the bath is provided by the *sento* or neighborhood public bath. In the old days everyone went to the *sento*. Now most Japanese have baths in their own homes but a few bathhouses survive in most urban areas, serving the needs of students, the poor, the nostalgic and people on the move.

You can identify the *sento* by its high chimney, often belching black smoke. For some visitors these chimneys confirm their worst fears about Japan's lack of zoning laws, but they are only helping to keep the water hot. As soon as you're through the *noren* (curtain) at the entrance, you divide by sex, men going into one changing room, women another. You pay a standard charge of ¥260, plus a ¥20 surcharge if you wash your hair. Undress, leaving your clothes in a basket or locker, and go through glass doors to the bathing area, also segregated by sex. Then simply follow the etiquette described above. You will have to put up with some staring, particularly if you are hairy, but you may get into some interesting conversations. Enjoy the naive painting of Mt. Fuji or another countrified scene on the back wall.

Some *sento*, notably in working class sections of big cities, are still flourishing. One in the Jujo section of Tokyo stays open to 1 a.m., and is enlivened around midnight by the arrival of the local *kabuki* troupe, still in their make-up.

Sauna baths have caught on in Japan in a big way, and Tokyo has a number of all-night saunas. The city's many Turkish baths have recently been persuaded to change their name to 'Soapland'. Numbering some 1,800 nationwide, they sprang up in the wake of the 1956 Anti-Prostitution Law -- and it wasn't a coincidence. See **Tokyo at Night** for more on that subject.

FOOD

'Like being bitten to death by butterflies', the reaction of one Westerner to *kabuki*, might apply equally to a first experience with Japanese food. At its classical best it is extremely pretty, like *kabuki*, and consists of a large number of different tiny dishes which all appear on the table, properly a low one on *tatami* mats, at the same time. The visitor doesn't have a clue where to begin. Mouthful by dainty mouthful there's a lot of food there, but does it amount to a meal?

The answer, frankly, is no. Just as the English word 'meal' also means the edible part of a grain, the Japanese word '*gohan*' also means rice -- strictly 'honorable rice'. Until very recently most Japanese ate rice three times a day, and it is still the basis of their diet. Boiled until the grains, while still distinct, stick together so that it can be easily eaten with chopsticks, it is served absolutely plain -- no salt, no butter, nothing. When one newcomer poured soy sauce over his rice in a Tokyo restaurant the waitress took it away and brought him another bowl, assuming he had done so by mistake.

Despite its plainness it is not a lowly

Exterior of a bar-cum-restaurant in Tokyo. The rustic-looking facade has simply been stuck on to the workaday concrete of the building behind.

food. The peasant who was so poor he had to eat a substitute such as nourishing and delicious sweet potatoes was considered pitiable indeed. Rice is the food of emperors, as the paddy field in the grounds of the Imperial Palace, ceremoniously planted by the emperor each year, attests.

The basic Japanese meal consists of rice, soup (either *miso shiru*, made of fermented soybean paste, or a consomme type), and *kazu*. *Kazu* translates inadequately as 'side dishes', and it means everything which is neither rice nor soup. If one of these elements is missing, it's not a real meal.

The guest surveys the many weird and wonderful dishes littering the table in front of him but finds to his perplexity neither rice nor soup. The reason is that, like the lengthy and complicated rituals that precede the wrestling in a sumo bout, these *kazu* are only a prelude to the real business of the meal.

Once his eye has been charmed and his palate teased and tickled by the preparations of raw tuna, wild mountain vegetables, chilled *tofu* with ginger and *shiso* leaf, deep-fried pumpkin and lotus root, mushrooms and shrimp set in custard, once his brain has been fired by good sake, then at last it is time for his stomach to assert itself. The strong drink is cleared away and replaced by tea and in come the rice and soup and a bowl of pickled vegetables.

He can fill up with as many bowlfuls of rice as he likes, and the soup will be replenished at the same time.

The ideal life, according to Japanese folk-wisdom, consists of eating Chinese food in a French house attended by a Japanese wife. Many people, including visitors from abroad who have eaten their way through the initial difficulties, would gladly substitute Japanese food for Chinese. Bland it is, certainly compared with the fiery flavors of southern Asia. Tasteless it is not. Low in cholesterol and animal fats it is at its best, and with reservations (see below), very healthy food. And its variety is mind-boggling.

The very best place to sample a meal of the type described above is at the home of a reasonably traditional and reasonably affluent Japanese family. Failing that, *kaiseki-ryori* restaurants offer Japanese cuisine at its grandest and most elaborate. The food will gen-

ABOVE Tokyo *Yakitoriya* office workers rake over the day's business.

70

erally be served on trays in a private *tatami* room, and the bill will be high. **Tsujitome** in Ginza (tel: (03) 573-5226) is a *kaiseki-ryori* restaurant with a good reputation.

The Oriental Carnivore

Sukiyaki (pronounced '*ski-yaki*') and *shabu-shabu* are the Japanese dishes most commonly offered to foreign visitors. They are delicious but much meatier than traditional Japanese cuisine. Buddhist tradition and the lack of pasture land meant that until recent times the only meat the Japanese ate in any quantity was whale, they obtained most of their protein from fish and from soybean foods such as *tofu* and *miso*. In 1872 the Meiji emperor first tasted beef and pronounced it fine, and attitudes have been changing steadily ever since. Meat is nonetheless very expensive.

Sukiyaki consists of thinly sliced beef cooked at the table with onions, mushrooms and other vegetables, jelly-like *konnyaku* or *shirataki* and *tofu*, in a delicious broth of stock, soy sauce and sweet sake. *Shabu-shabu* is similarly thin-sliced beef cooked by each individual diner by dipping it for a few moments in a pan of boiling water then dunking it in a soy-based dipping sauce before eating. Finally *udon* -- wheat flour noodles -- are cooked in the boiling water and similarly dunked, in place of rice. *Shabu-shabu* is an onomatopoeic word which is supposed to suggest the sound of the beef hitting the boiling water -- 'slap-slap'.

Suehiro in Ginza, tel: (03) 570-0624, is a famed *sukiyaki* joint with many branches elsewhere. They are also famous for their steak, which is expensive and fatty but very tender. If it is advertised as Kobe beef -- Kobe being a port city near Kyoto -- you can be confident about its quality: the Kobe animals are pampered to death rather than slaughtered, fed with preboiled mash and bottles of beer and massaged by the farmer's family.

Seryna in Roppongi, tel: (03) 403-6211, is renowned for its *shabu-shabu*.

Frying Tonight

Tempura, another favorite with visitors, is the Japanese answer to fish and chips, less chips. The basic idea arrived with the Portuguese in the sixteenth century and has been Japanized into a crisp, deep-fried delicacy. Items which drop, fresh and battered, into the deep fat include aubergines, *shiso* leaves, slices of lotus root and carrot, as well as shrimp, *kisu* and many other types of fish. Presented to the customer on absorbent paper which soaks up the grease, it is dipped in a soy-based broth before eating.

An expensive but highly recommended tempura restaurant is **Ten-Ichi Honten** in Ginza, tel: (03) 571-1949. A much cheaper place, also recommended, is **Tsuruoka** in Minato-ku, tel: (03) 408-4061.

The Raw Reality

As an island country, fish has been central to the Japanese diet for centuries, and when you enter a *sushi* shop you are in one of the most popular shrines of the national culture. Due to the recent spread of Japanese restaurants around the world, raw fish is not the object of shock and horror that it once was. As with many alien foods -- frogs' legs, snails -- most of the difficulty is in the mind. Once the first sliver of really good *maguro* (tuna) has melted on your tongue and slithered down your gullet, objections will evaporate in the sake fumes.

Sashimi is raw fish plain and simple, dipped in soy sauce flavored with *wasabi* (fiery-flavored Japanese horseradish). *Nigirizushi* are slices of raw fish, shellfish, shrimp or sweet Japanese omelet, laid on thumb-sized portions of sweetened, vinegared rice and presented in pairs. Similarly dunked -- it's okay to use your fingers -- it is eaten in one bite, then the mouth is freshened in preparation for the next pair with a slice of ginger. Oversize mugs of green tea accompany your *sashimi* or *sushi*, unless you are drinking sake or beer in which case the tea will come at the end.

Sushi shops come in all grades of quality from brilliant to rotten. There are even shops, not recommended, where the food comes round on a little conveyer belt and you take what you fancy. For the first experience it's wise to blow some money to avoid disappointment. Why not treat yourself to a bite at **Kiku-Zushi** in Nishi-Shinjuku, tel: (03) 361-4043, one of the best -- though not one of the most expensive -- *sushi* shops in town.

Japanese Roulette

One fish eaten *sashimi*-style, though only at restaurants which specialize in it, is *fugu* or *blowfish*. The liver and ovaries of *fugu* contain a deadly poison, one ounce of which could kill a man in minutes. Nowadays *fugu* chefs are all licensed by the government and deaths are rare. Has this done away with the fun? Some gourmets say so, maintaining that the slightly mouth-numbing effect of the poison (taken presumably in very small quantities) is part of the pleasure. *Fugu* is at its best -- and safest -- in the winter months, and is also eaten *nabe*-style, as part of a delicious stew. A good place to try it is **Ashibé** in Tsukiji, near Tokyo's fish market, tel: (03) 543-3540; they also serve turtle cuisine (*suppon*). As the *fugu* here is fresh it is only served between the end of October and March.

Brown Grains

One of the reservations about the

healthiness of Japanese food derives from the fact that, in common with other Asians, the Japanese polish the raw grains of rice until they are gleaming white, removing in the process all the vital Vitamin B. Poignant evidence of the national fixation with 'pure', 'clean' white rice is to be found in Ibuse Masuji's great novel about Hiroshima after the bomb, *Black Rain*, in which the protagonists, although practically on the verge of starvation, meticulously polish their miserable rice ration grain by grain as a way of maintaining their dignity.

Modern Japanese know that brown rice is good for the health but the great majority still shuns it. A rare exception is the delicious **Tenmi** vegetarian restaurant in Shibuya, tel: (03) 496-9703. Vegetarian *tempura* and *ofukuro-no-aji* ('flavors of mother') are two excellent dishes served here, and the shop downstairs sells organically grown, chemical-free brown rice (*genmai*) and vegetables.

(The other reservation about the healthiness of traditional Japanese food is that it contains too much salt, and this is supposed to be responsible for the high incidence of cerebral haemorrhage as a cause of death. If you are worried about this, avoid eating too many pickles and splashing soy sauce on everything.)

Unblemished Bean

Tofu -- soybean curd -- is a food which has had an enormous impact in the West during the past decade. Served chilled in summer, stewed in winter, deep-fried, stuffed or diced in soups, it is a vital part of the Japanese diet, and much more highly regarded by gourmets than its low price (and the rather infradig things that get done to

The multitude of red lanterns drive the message home: this is a cheap place to eat and drink.

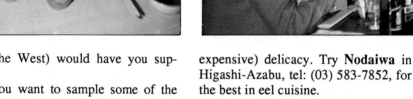

it in the West) would have you suppose.

If you want to sample some of the many marvelous ways in which it is served, visit the delightful **Sasanoyuki** restaurant in Negishi, tel: (03) 873-1145, and admire the lovely garden at the same time.

Nothing To Do With Cats!

Visit the kitchen to check if you like -- *tonkatsu* has nothing to do with cats. *Ton* means 'pork' and *katsu* is a contraction of 'cutlet'. *Tonkatsu* is deep-fried pork cutlet, served either on a bed of rice *domburi*-style or as part of a *teishoku* (set meal) with raw cabbage, slices of lemon, *miso* soup and rice. At a good shop it's great. One such is **Hirano-ya**, tel: (03) 275-2847, in the underground shopping complex under the Yaesu-guchi side of Tokyo station.

Other cheap and popular *domburi*-style dishes are *oyakodon* (literally 'parent-and-child' *domburi*, a mixture of chicken and egg) and *unaju* (broiled eel). Prepared well, eel is a great (and

expensive) delicacy. Try **Nodaiwa** in Higashi-Azabu, tel: (03) 583-7852, for the best in eel cuisine.

At the Sign of the Red Lantern

A red paper lantern hanging outside a restaurant -- or outside a little cart -- means *nomi-ya*, 'drinking shop'. But the Japanese never drink without eating at the same time, and that doesn't mean just peanuts. *Tsumami* is the word for an appetizer accompanying beer or sake -- be careful not to say '*tsunami*' which is a tidal wave caused by an earthquake -- and they come in all shapes and sizes.

At the **Nombe** chain, for example, which has 32 branches in Tokyo, appetizers include *atsuage* (deep-fried *tofu*), *nikuzume* (green peppers stuffed with meat) and *wakame-su* (vinegared seaweed salads). Add such items as fried chicken, *kawa-ebi* (fried shrimp) and *nabe-mono* (stew like foods, marvelously warming in winter) and it's easy to see that your appetizer can swell into a full-blown meal. If it does, you may feel like finishing up with *o-*

74

chazuke, boiled rice with pickled sour plum, *nori*, (seaweed) and peppery spices, with hot green tea poured over the whole lot. This dish is customarily prepared by long-suffering wives to help their tipsy husbands sober up, but you can enjoy it just as well in a restaurant.

The telephone number of the Ebisu branch of Nombe is (03) 464-9441.

Yakitori is a rough delicacy you will also find at the sign of the red lantern. *Yakitori-ya* restaurants, found by the dozen close to major railway stations in office areas such as Shibuya, Shinjuku and Yurakucho, are perhaps the closest Japanese equivalent to the English pub: down-to-earth, noisy, cheerful and relatively cheap. *Yakitori* are bits of chicken and other fowl such as quail, duck and sparrow, often taken from highly improbable parts of the bird's body, spitted on a stick, dipped in sauce and barbecued.

No particular *yakitori-ya* cries out to be recommended and phone numbers are beside the point. Just head for that friendly looking joint crowded with flush-faced salarymen and find a seat. Pointing to likely looking items being devoured by the people around you is a quite acceptable way to order.

Another cheap and cheerful dish worth knowing about is *okonomiyaki*, a favorite with students. It is a sort of do-it-yourself filled omelette. The waiter brings the ingredients of the meal, which might include cuttlefish and vegetables as well as egg, and the diners cook for themselves on the hotplate built into the table.

Ye Olde Farmhouse

The atmosphere of an old country farmhouse in the middle of Tokyo -- that's what the popular *robata-yaki* restaurants offer. Surrounded by tasteful reminders of country life -- straw raincoats, bamboo snow-shoes, old farming implements -- the diners sit at a counter or

A passion for food: FAR LEFT elegant *bento-*(lunch box) style dinner in Kyoto, CENTER a *teppanyaki* restaurant in Tokyo, RIGHT a do-it-yourself *okonomiyaki* restaurant.

around an old wooden hearth. Like the hostelries described above, the focus of interest at *robata-yaki* is drinking, but the tsumami at the *robata* (grill) are varied and appetizing and may include whale steaks, shellfish, *miso*-topped aubergines and bamboo shoots. All the evening's ingredients are displayed at the counter (as in a *sushi* shop) so if you sit there you can order merely by pointing. And after it has been cooked, the dish of your choice may arrive on the end of a paddle with an immensely long handle. A recommended *robata-yaki* is **Robata-Honten** in Yurakucho tel: (03) 591-1905.

In most modern *robata-yaki* the grill is gas-fired. A rare example of a restaurant which employs real charcoal is the tiny **Dengaku** in Kamakura tel: (0467) 23-2121, just over an hour from central Tokyo. It is barely larger than the average Western bathroom, but the fish, vegetables and *tofu* cooked over the flames are unbeatable.

Setting 'Em Up

Whatever the *nomi-ya* you wind up in, an embarrassment of choice is not going to be one of your problems in the matter of drink, at least. Beer, sake and whiskey -- these are the three options, wherever you go.

Beer means the excellent Japanese-made lager which has been going down the hatch here for 100 years and more. All brands are drinkable but Kirin is the most popular, while Yebisu is probably the best. Some firms market draft beer in bottles, a paradox which has confounded even the most subtle Japanologists.

Sake is the national drink: Chinese who visited Japan nearly two millennia ago noted that the Japanese were getting stoned on it even then. In those days the fermentation was set in motion by having shrine virgins chew mouthfuls of rice then spit the mushy result into casks, where the enzyme in human saliva set to work. Conditions of hygiene have improved a lot since then, but the price has gone up too. The protection offered for political reasons to Japanese farmers means that Japanese rice is three times the price it is anywhere else in the world, and sake is as a result a good deal more expensive than beer, which is mostly made from im-

ported barley.

It's a splendid tipple all the same. Taken hot in the winter it is wonderfully warming, though the best quality sake may be drunk cold in all seasons. If you don't mix it with other drinks, it should leave you with an uncannily clear head the next morning.

If it doesn't, you were probably drinking in a cheap place where the sake is cut, quite legally, with industrial alcohol and other additives to reduce the price. Sake made with rice and nothing else accounts for only one percent of national production, and most of that is made in small breweries in the country.

Sake sold in liquor stores in large *issho* bottles containing about half a gallon comes in three grades of quality: *tokkyu* (special class), *ikkyu* (first class) and *nikyu* (second class). Sweet sake is called *amakuchi*; the dry variety which most Westerners prefer is called *karakuchi*. If you are keen to try 100 per cent rice sake ask for *kome hyaku-pa-cento*.

The history of Japanese whisky goes back to the beginning of this century. The best is fine, and contains a considerable proportion of malt whisky, imported in bulk from Scotland. Most Japanese drink it as *mizuwari* with ice and lots of water. Many pubs and 'snacks' operate a keep-bottle system: the customer buys a bottle of whiskey and writes his name on the label, and can come back and tipple from it whenever he likes, paying only for ice and appetizers.

A Bowl of Surprises

Your first glimpse of a bowl of *oden* may set you wondering all over again about that famed aesthetic sense of the Japanese. It's the funniest collection of things: triangles of grey jelly; long, hollow, fleshy tubes, hard-boiled eggs and bundles of seaweed, presented in a thin soup with a smear of mustard on the side of the bowl. It is in effect a vegetarian (or semi-) stew, and the least you can say for it is that it warms you up.

Kamaboko a bland, usually white

Two approaches to *tofu*: OPPOSITE a *yudofu* restaurant in Kyoto, and ABOVE the intimate *Dengaku* in Kamakura, where *tofu*, fish and vegetables are grilled over charcoal.

'fish sausage', is behind several of the specialities, including the above-mentioned tubes (*chikuwa*). The gray jelly is *konnyaku*, a nutritious food made from a sort of powdered arrowroot. Another treat is *takarabukuro*, 'treasure bags' made from deep-fried *tofu* and filled with translucent noodles and other surprises.

Probably the best and most appropriate place to try *oden* is in one of those tiny, portable, tent-like bars which are to be found in the streets near mainline stations in busy parts of Tokyo and elsewhere. Make your selection from the bubbling pans of *oden* by pointing and wash it down with beer or cheap, hot sake. Relish the fragile coziness of the place as the world buzzes about its business just the other side of the cotton walls.

An *oden-ya* (*oden* shop) with the great bonus of an illustrated menu with English and romanized captions is to be found in the Dotonb ori section of Osaka. Check Osaka in **Japan: The Broad Highway**, below, for details.

Noodles Fat and Thin

Noodles are Japan's very own fast food. The infamous instant Cup Noodle has wormed its way onto supermarket shelves all over the West, but don't let that prejudice you. There are many more palatable variants.

Soba are gray-colored buckwheat noodles made with a base of buckwheat flour. Handmade and with a high proportion of buckwheat, they transcend the fast-food category, and some of the restaurants that specialize in *soba* are quite fancy.

Udon are fat white noodles made from wheat flour.

Ramen are fine yellow Chinese-derived noodles.

The common way of eating all three types is in large bowls of steaming stock with trimmings such as fish or shrimp *tempura* or slices of beef.

Slurping is *de rigueur* and makes the noodles taste better. In summer, *soba* is often served cold on a bamboo screen, to be dunked into a cold sauce before eating, and similar treatment befalls a type of very fine white noodle called *somen*. The cloudy liquid in that lacquerware teapot which arrives with the cold *soba* is the water it was boiled in. When you've finished eating, pour this hot water into what remains of your dunking sauce and quaff it. It's good.

Homesickness
Western-style restaurants abound in Tokyo, but in the vast majority Japanese cooks prepare Western food for Japanese taste buds. It may be good, but it may not be what you had in mind.

There are an increasing number of exceptions to this rule, offering the discerning (and the homesick) something approaching the real thing. A few examples:

FRENCH. L'ecrin Ginza, Ginza Mikimoto Pearl Building. The chef de cuisine is a member of France's prestigious Academie Culinaire. Superb food. Tel: (03) 462-1591. **Rengaya** Hillside Terrace, Daikanyama. Paul Bocuse's Tokyo restaurant is a little way off the beaten track, but the Lyon cuisine on offer makes it worth it. Tel: (03) 462-1591.

ITALIAN. La Cometa, Azabu Juban. A very cosy restaurant serving authentic Italian fish and meat dishes. Tel: (03) 470-5105.

INDIAN. Moti, Roppongi and Akasaka. Arguably the best Indian restaurants in

Sake, the national drink. LEFT Large wooden tubs of it, decoratively labelled and tied up with rice straw. ABOVE LEFT The first stage: rice fermenting at a small sake brewery in Takayama. ABOVE RIGHT The last stage: a mama-san dispenses the finished product in a high-class bar in the same town.

79

Japan. Delicious tandoori dishes, *sagh*, piping hot *nan*. Tel: Roppongi (03) 479-1939, 479-1955; Akasaka (03) 582-3620, 584-3760.

CHINESE (Peking-style). There are many authentic Chinese restaurants in the Tokyo area, with the densest concentration in Yokohama's Chinatown. **Hokkai-en**, however, is near the center of town in Nishi-Azabu (tel: (03) 407-8507) and is one of the best Peking-style joints in the capital.

THAI. Chiang Mai offers real Thai cuisine, fiendishly hot and otherwise, in intimate surroundings in Yurakucho, tel: (03) 580-0456.

Eating On the Move

A special treat unique to Japan is the *eki-ben* or station lunch-box. Japanese food fits the lunch-box format well: small quantities of a variety of different things agreeably presented. *Makunouchi-bento* is the version most commonly found nationwide and typically consists of small pieces of fried chicken and seafood, *kamaboko* (fish paste sausage), *shumai* (Chinese-style meat dumplings), boiled or vinegared vegetables, pickles and a field of boiled rice with a pickled plum (*umeboshi*) dead center suggesting the Japanese flag.

But many other types are encountered when traveling, some presented in charming wooden cases or ceramic pots. Just ask for '*bento*' on the platform of any large station, study the photographs of the contents on display and try your luck. It's the cheapest and arguably the best way of eating on the move.

Problems

The only serious problem for the adventurous gourmet out and about in Japan is language. Many is the time the grateful visitor has opened a menu, on the cover of which the restaurant's name and the word MENU are boldly printed in flawless English, only to find that the dishes themselves are described only in flawless Japanese.

There is usually a way out of this fix. A great many restaurants have wax or plastic replicas of the food on offer displayed in the window. Just take the waitress out to the front and point. Pointing, this time at the actual ingredients, is also recommended in *sushi* shops and *robata-yaki* (though in the former there may be models of set dinners to help you as well). Sit at the counter as close as possible to the man in charge.

If there is nothing to point at and no one is willing to help you out, retire with dignity and, if it smells as if it's worth it, resolve to return to fight again another day with your secret weapon -- a Japanese-speaking companion.

However warm and helpful the service, don't leave a tip on the table: more than likely your waiter will come haring down the street after you to return it. Tipping is not the custom in Japan.

OPPOSITE PAGE Bottles of sake outside a small brewery in Takayama. ABOVE, LEFT A Chinese restaurant in Yokohama's Chinatown. ABOVE RIGHT The two-minute meal: noodles - *soba* and *udon* - in broth are served from stands like this on many station platforms: cheap, hot, and just about palatable.

Japan: The Broad Highway

TOKYO: THE CITY AND BEYOND

If you've just arrived in Japan, you are probably in Tokyo. You know all the bad things already -- the smog, the crowds, the 'rabbit hutches' people live in. Now for the good news: it's safe, it's friendly and it's one of the most energetic -- and energizing -- cities in the world. It's much less smoggy than it was, and fish are returning to the rivers. There are not enough parks, but a couple of hours from the center there are volcanoes, lakes and primeval forests. Now read on.

'EASTERN CAPITAL'

With a population of nearly 12,000,000, Tokyo vies with Shanghai as the largest city in the world. For population density it has few competitors, for chaotic lack of planning none. One glimpse can be enough to send new arrivals scuttling back into the hotel lobby.

It's important to remember that this monster doesn't bite. It's both harmless and wholesome. You can, and probable will, lose your way within moments -- the idea of using street names was introduced by the Americans after the war but never caught on -- but no harm will befall you. You can't read the signs, you can't ask the way, you feel as helpless as a toddler -- but, despite the frenzied activity, there are thousands of people out there ready to guide you gently on your way. As capital cities go, Tokyo is remarkably friendly.

This friendliness seems to be bound up with its lack of any rational plan. The city has been almost entirely razed to the ground twice this century, once in the 1923 earthquake, once in the bombing of 1945. Both times it was rebuilt at top speed without any sem-blance of overall planning. Both times this was deplored by architects and many other enlightened people as a shocking waste of opportunity. Both times it probably saved the city's soul.

Why? Because the human fabric of the city has managed to survive these waves of destruction almost intact . Tokyo consists of the dozens of villages which once dotted the Kanto Plain. Despite the destruction, despite the immigrants who still flood in from all over the country, the village feeling persists, sometimes almost as far as to the city center.

The Past

The Kanto Plain which Tokyo dominates is the largest area of fairly flat land in Japan, but it was developed much later in the nation's history than the smaller plains around Kyoto and Nara. As in most Japanese towns, the nucleus was a castle, and the first one was built here in the fifteenth century.

The first Tokugawa shogun made Edo, the city's old name, his capital in the sixteenth century, and it began to expand rapidly, gobbling up without quite destroying many surrounding villages in the process.

Edo was the *de facto* capital throughout the 250 years of the Tokugawa period. The capital in name, however, was still Kyoto. In 1867 the shogun was

---

ABOVE Tokyo is full of extreme architectural contrasts.

deposed and the emperor restored to his former position of prestige. He moved with his court to Edo Castle and the city was renamed Tokyo -- 'Eastern Capital'. Expansion continued apace.

A British envoy who visited the city at that time praised it as one of the most beautiful in the Orient. This century's earthquakes and bombs have ensured that this compliment is unlikely to be repeated, unfortunately, and the city has few buildings of great antiquity or his-

torical interest.

But it is very much the hub of the nation -- more so than many capitals -- and it is the best and biggest showcase for the new Japan: for the electronics, the motorbikes, the cars, the fashion, the architecture. It has the most museums and galleries, the best stores, the best theaters and cinemas, many of the best restaurants and the most exciting and varied night life in the country.

Where shall we start?

The Hub of the Hub

The **Imperial Palace** in the center of the city is one of the few historical musts for the tourist, but you can't see much of it because the emperor still lives there. Reliable sources say it is

ABOVE *Hi-no-maru* ('round sun') flags wave for the emperor on his birthday. RIGHT The Imperial Palace moat, interface between the world of the court and the business section of Marunouchi.

considerably harder to penetrate than Buckingham Palace. You can admire the moat which surrounds it and the massive stones of the outer walls. Admire, too, the white walls of the palace itself, though temper your admiration with the knowledge that they were recently rebuilt in ferro-concrete.

The **East Garden**, across one of two bridges from the Plaza, is open to the public daily between 9 a.m. and 3 p.m. except Mondays and Fridays. If you want a closer look, the palace itself throws open its gates on two days a year, 29 April (the emperor's birthday) and 2 January, 9 a.m. to 3.30 p.m. Hibiya station is the best subway stop for the palace.

Important museums and halls are located near the palace. Near Takebashi (Takebashi subway) are the **National Museums of Modern Art, Science and Craft**. The **National Theater** is diametrically opposite Takebashi on the other side of the palace

(Nagata-cho subway), while near Kudanshita subway is the massive **Nippon Budokan** hall, the main Tokyo venue for visiting big-name rock bands when it is not hosting tournaments of judo and kendo.

The large area between the palace and Nihombashi is the business heart of the city and is as smart and sterile as one would expect. Linger not, except to sample **Steinmetz's** delicious pumpkin pies near the north exit of Tokyo station (Yaesu-guchi side) and the

English-language bookshop on the third floor of **Maruzen** (Nihombashi subway). In the area of Nihombashi, by the way, lived William Adams, the first (only?) English samurai and model for the hero of James Clavell's novel *Shogun*.

The Silver Mint
The **Ginza** ('Silver Mint') area southeast of the palace (Ginza subway) is the swishiest, sleekest part of town and has

been in the forefront of things for a century or more. Tokyo's first trams and subways ran here, and this was where the smart set came to drink coffee and show off their Western-style umbrellas and watches.

Now it's where the élite salaryman comes to put his entertainment account to proper use in some of the world's most expensive hostess clubs. Those using their own money are advised to be careful in this area and to check prices before ordering, or they could wind up paying several thousand yen for a single drink.

Emerge from the subway at **4-chome** crossing: the **Wako** jewellery establishment and the **Mitsukoshi** department store are typical of Ginza's huge and sophisticated attractions. It's often hard to get your bearings in this area: ask a friendly face, '*Sony Biru doko?*' ('Where is the Sony building?') and move in the direction indicated. In the sidestreets you pass on your left are smart little boutiques, coffee shops, clubs and restaurants and occasionally, if you look hard enough, a stubborn old traditional shop selling authentic craftware. The **Sony Building** itself has demonstration models of all the famous electronic company's current equipment.

Back on the main drag (**Harumi Dori**), and going in the same direction, you run into a warren of little shops near the Yamanote line known collectively as **Sukiyabashi Shopping Center** and offering all manner of tax-free electronic goods, watches and so on. The people who work there are used to foreign customers and are helpful. **Akihabara**, however, is probably cheaper (see below).

Down at the other end of Chuo Dori, beyond Higashi-Ginza station, is the ornately Oriental ferro-concrete of the **Kabuki-za**, while further still is the **Tsukiji Fish Market**. The *sushi* shops around here are, reasonably enough,

among the best in Tokyo.

Stiffer and Looser

Edge round to the south of our original hub, the palace, and you enter another pleasure zone. **Akasaka** is both stiffer and looser than Ginza: stiffer in the north where the **Diet** (Parliament) convenes; looser in the west, behind Aka-saka-Mitsuke station, where the young and beautiful dance the night away at discos like **Mugen** and **Byblos**.

It's a handy area to boogie in, being

only a short stumble to several of the city's top hotels (New Otani, Hilton,Tokyu...) and bed. But be careful you don't get run over by a rickshaw: a few geishas still practice their soothing arts close by.

The Outsider

The outsider, craning and jostling for position -- that' s how **Roppongi** ('Six Trees') looks on the map in relation to the areas described above. And it's true: Roppongi is younger, crazier, later, noisier -- and a little cheaper than elsewhere.

Practically surrounded by embassies, Roppongi has been a favorite hang-out of Tokyo's foreign community for many years, but its transformation into one of the centers of the city's youth culture is a more recent event. The *gaijin* (foreigner) presence remains strong, however, and with models, whiz kids and embassy people thronging cheerfully together on the streets, it's almost like being back in the West.

Start your tour from **Almond** coffee shop near Roppongi station and walk

towards **Tokyo Tower**. Most of what matters around here is on, or behind,this main street, and it includes discos, English- and American-style bars, live jazz spots and international (genuinely international) restaurants. Some of Tokyo's most startling and inspiring modern pop architecture is to be found here and in Kamiyacho, next door.

OPPOSITE AND ABOVE Scenes in Ginza, central Tokyo's long-established playground for the fashionable.

火傷しそうなクリスマス。

TOP A Ginza sandwich-board man advertizes a club with '*naisu gyaru*' (nice girls); BELOW Citizens wait patiently for the walking green. RIGHT 'Life is a party' declares this Ginza shop window. The traditional granny seems unconvinced.

人生はパーティ。82·X'mas.

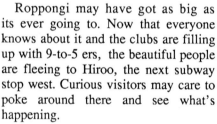

Roppongi may have got as big as its ever going to. Now that everyone knows about it and the clubs are filling up with 9-to-5 ers, the beautiful people are fleeing to Hiroo, the next subway stop west. Curious visitors may care to poke around there and see what's happening.

High and Low

On the opposite side of the subway map from the places we have been touring so far is **Shinjuku**, a Tokyo parvenu on the grand scale. Shinjuku station is the biggest in the country, and one of the most bewildering, although people will tell you, if you complain, that it is quite straightforward really.

The station is the dividing line between Shinjuku's two utterly different sections. On the west is a cluster of brand-new skyscrapers, the background for innumerable commercials and the symbol of the hopes of (some) Tokyoites for their city's future. Attractions for visitors include some good, high restaurants, staggering views

and, in the basement of the Sumitomo Building, the **Do Sports Plaza**, one of the few places in Japan where you can play squash (among many other things).

East of the station, on the other hand, is one of Tokyo's most lushly low-life quarters. Dozens and dozens of tiny bars and restaurants skirt the station; beyond spread whole tracts of porno cinemas, strip clubs, gay bars and more. There's a strong gangster (*yakuza*) presence here, and it is one of the few parts of town that can on occasion turn nasty, but compared with similar sections of most other cities in the

world it is still extremely innocuous. In Kabuki-cho, unlike almost everywhere else in Tokyo, the action goes on all night, and is as crowded at 4 a.m. as at 9 p.m.

On the more sober-sided main street, still on the east side, are several department stores and the excellent **Kinokuniya** book store -- foreign books are on the 5th floor. Try visiting on a Sunday: like the Ginza area, the main street is closed to traffic on that day and it's a good chance to observe Japanese youth at play without risking a carbon monoxide swoon.

Rocking Round the Shrine

An even better chance is provided on Sundays at **Harajuku**, a couple of stops down the Yamanote line, where hordes of trendy teenagers, known as *Takenokozoku* -- the Bamboo-shoot Gang -- jive away the afternoon to tapes of antiquated rock'n'roll.

If you get a headache trying to work out the sociological implications of this one, soothe it in the lovely grounds of

Meiji Shrine. This and neighboring **Yoyogi Park** form Tokyo's most spacious areas of green, and the shrine, though less than a century old, is classically simple and elegant. The shrine's association with the growth of State Shinto, the ideology behind the Japanese militarism of the 1930s, is the only thing that might cast a shadow over one's enjoyment of the place. The completion recently of a grandiose new entrance to the shrine fuels suspicion that rightist forces are pushing hard for a revival of the dangerous cult.

The area east of the shrine was remodeled in the early 1960s for the benefit of the athletes who came to the 1964 Tokyo Olympics and it is green and spacious. Walk down boulevard-like Omote-Sando towards the subway

OPPOSITE, LEFT Window-cleaner. ABOVE West Shinjuku's skyscrapers: solidly built, haphazardly arranged. St. Mary's Cathedral. OPPOSITE, BELOW by Kenzo Tange, Japan's most famous architect.

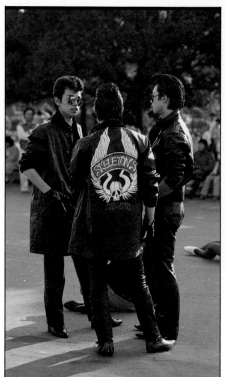

Tokyo Metropolitan Fine Art Museum. The park in which they are set has many cherry trees and is a favorite spot for cherry blossom viewing (*hanami*). Thousands of people gather under the trees during early April and -- write poems? meditate? think great thoughts? No: they drink, dance and roar with laughter. It's a great sight, and if you play your cards right you will be invited to join in.

Get back on the Yamanote line and

station of the same name. Two-thirds of the way down on the right is the **Oriental Bazaar**, one of Tokyo's best shops for traditional goods of every description, stocked with foreign preferences in mind. Buy all your souvenirs here and you will be able to persuade your friends that the Japanese still wear two swords and a topknot.

Old Town

Another nice park, and a mecca of museums, is to be found at **Ueno**, a few stops north of Tokyo on the Yamanote line. The museums include the **Tokyo National Museum** and the

go two stops south towards Tokyo station: here is **Akihabara**, famous the world over for cut-price electronic goods. The prices are low -- some say the lowest in the world -- and the quality is high. The only danger is of buying an appliance which will not work back home without adjustment -- or at all. Many salesmen speak some English, but why not have someone at

OPPOSITE Tribal fashions in Tokyo and Yokohama. ABOVE Elvis fans living to tapes of the King on a Sunday in Harajuku. CENTER Leafy Omote-Sando Boulevard nearby, closed to traffic on Sundays.

the front desk of your hotel write out this anxiety in Japanese, just in case?

Not far from here, at the far end of the Ginza subway line, is one of the few places in Tokyo with some of the charm and atmosphere that much of the city must have possessed before modernization. **Asakusa** it's called; to the foreign tongue it is readily confused with Akasaka, but they are worlds apart.

The main attraction is the **Asakusa Kannon Temple**, with its huge red

lantern and the tiny image of the goddess of mercy enshrined in it, and the long avenue of shops and stalls, many selling beautifully made traditional goods, which lead to it. It's worth setting aside a few hours to browse through this area at leisure, and to marvel at the changes that have come over the capital in a century.

This is the first temple we have had cause to mention in Tokyo. Temples -- tranquil, removed from the city bustle, often set at the foot of steep green hills -- seem at odds with Tokyo's raucous, cheery character. It's somehow appro-

priate that the Asakusa Temple should be the focus of a huge market, and that the temple's most famous emblem, the red lantern, should also be the customary sign for a bar.

Stranded the far side of the Yamanote loop line, Asakusa bustles less madly than elsewhere in Tokyo, but has far more than its share of excellent traditional restaurants.

Tokyo Disneyland

California is now only a 25-minute sub-

way ride from the center of Tokyo. In April 1983 Walt Disney Productions' third theme park, and the first outside the United States, opened its gates to the public. The huge amusement park, built on reclaimed land in Chiba, east of the city, is 1-1/2 times the size of the original in Anaheim, but its attractions are basically the same. The park's 58 hectare (114-acre) area is divided into four 'themed lands': Adventureland, Westernland, Fantasyland and Tomorrowland. Within each of these environments are a number of rides, including a jungle cruise, a trip through Snow

White's adventures and the much-praised space trip. The park is also crammed with performance areas, shops, cafés and restaurants, each carefully harmonized with the setting in which it is located.

The bad news for homesick Americans is that Tokyo Disneyland's lingua franca is Japanese. The good news, perhaps, is that the food available will at least be roughly similar to that at the original. The surprise for anybody unfamiliar with Disneyland in

relatively slack, and they also suggest that visitors consider eating before or after the regular lunch hour (12 noon to 1 p.m. in Japan): the queues outside the restaurants can be horrendous, and picnic lunches are not allowed inside the grounds. Admission cost ¥2,500; a 'Big Ten Ticket Book', which includes the cost of admission and a choice of ten rides, costs ¥3,900.

To get to Tokyo Disneyland take the Tozai subway line from Otemachi or Nihombashi to Urayasu, then the bus

America is the attention given to detail in making this a seamless and self-contained four-dimensional theater and the extravagantly high quality of the finish.

Fear of overcrowding led Tokyo Disneyland's management to stipulate, before the park opened, that all visitors must book in advance, but this policy has been abandoned as unnecessary. Now you are almost guaranteed entrance on any day in the year, though if it's really packed you may be asked to wait a while. The management point out that mornings and evenings are

from outside Urayasu station to the park's main entrance. Alternatively, take the shuttle bus which runs from the Yaesu side of Tokyo station. A JNR railway station right outside the front gate is scheduled for completion in the next couple of years.

OPPOSITE, LEFT AND ABOVE RIGHT Akihabara: wall-to-wall electrical and electronic goods stores. OPPOSITE, RIGHT Cinderella's Castle at Tokyo Disneyland, one of the city's newer landmarks. ABOVE LEFT Plastic blossoms and ornate lamps brighten an Asakusa side street.

Tourist Information

Yurakucho station is one stop south of Tokyo on the Yamanote line and here is the visitor's single most useful address: the **Tourist Information Center**. It's just two minutes from Yurakucho station on the way towards Hibiya Park (Hibiya Koen) or one minute from Hibiya station (subway) going towards Ginza. This is the place to go for maps and tour brochures. Also, although not on display, the TIC people have a large number of very reliable mini-guides, giving detailed and reliable information on a large number of tourist hot-spots. See **Travelers' Tips** for more on the TIC's services.

Touring Tokyo

Getting to know Tokyo's interesting ins and outs takes time. If you're in a hurry, why not join a tour? The Japan Travel Bureau (JTB) offers several with the foreign visitor in mind, and though the buses tend to get clogged in the capital's frightful traffic they will take you to places you would have trouble finding on your own. The following are the regular ones:

Art Around Town. Demonstrations of several traditional arts and crafts, including flower-arranging, tea ceremony, paper-folding and woodblock printing. Fare: ¥11,000, children 6-11 ¥9,000, with lunch. Every Monday.

Village Life and Crafts. Visits to toy-making and other craft workshops, a *bonsai* garden, and an association of farmers and fruit-growers. Fare as above. Every Wednesday.

Industrial Tokyo. Visits to a variety of factories and plants to watch the 'Japanese Miracle' in action, including computer laboratories and a car factory. Varied itineraries offered. Fare as above. Every Tuesday, Thursday and Friday.

Dynamic Tokyo. The basic getting-to-know Tokyo tour, calling at Tokyo Tower, Imperial East Garden or Imperial Palace Plaza, Asakusa Kannon Temple and Meiji Shrine. Fare: ¥16,000, children 6-11 ¥9,000, with lunch. Daily.

All the above tours depart from major hotels at 9 a.m. and return at 5.30 or 6 p.m. For night tours see below.

Tokyo at Night

Tokyo after dark is a bizarre world that fascinates, repels and bewilders all at once. The main streets are bright with some of the world's most extravagant neon, but it's down the winding, scruffy alleys near the big stations that the action seems to be happening. These streets were made with the night in mind. By day they may be mean, cheap, tawdry; at night they glow and buzz with life. They are dotted with fortune-tellers, erect and solemn before their little tables with lantern and charts. A smell of hot sake, soy sauce and barbecuing chicken blows out of that *yakitori-ya* on the corner where shirt-sleeved businessmen huddle on beer crates. Disco sounds bombard the street from one doorway where a man dressed up as a monkey is selling lottery tickets, while from an open window just around the corner come the staccato notes of a *shamisen*, like drops of hard rain hitting an iron roof one at a time. Gangs of boys and pretty girls spill out of a restaurant, pour into a club, laughing and kidding. A door slides open behind a little curtain, granting the briefest glimpse of a tiny 'snack' with a huge white grand piano.

It's all very strange and convivial. How can you join in?

If you like live rock or jazz, start with one of the capital's numerous live houses. **Ballantines 2**, (tel: (03) 478-5068), for example, in Roppongi's Ho-

sho Building, one minute from Roppongi station. There's live jazz, rock and fusion daily from 7 p.m. to midnight, and laser discs from then until 4 a.m. Tokyo is one of the best places in the world to hear jazz, and **Body and Soul** tel: (03) 408-2094, also close to Roppongi station, has some of Tokyo's best. It's open from 7 in the evening until 2 or 3 in the morning. **Crocodile** tel: (03) 499-5205 is a club not far from Harajuku station with amazing décor where you can hear rock-'n'roll from 8.30 p.m.

Mugen, tel: (03) 584-4481, and **Byblos** tel: (03) 584-4484 are two of the capital's best-known discos, next door to each other in Akasaka. But Roppongi's may have more style these days. Roppongi has whole buildings stacked with discos. Try **El Condor** in Roppongi Plaza Building tel: (03) 401-7478 or **Nirvana**, in Elsa Building tel: (03) 405-9904, both fashionable spots open late and both near Roppongi station.

We looked at *nomi-ya*, Japanese bars, in the **Food** section of the last chapter. Many close well before midnight. If you fancy staying up a little later, try a Western-style (or even Western-managed) bar. **The Rising Sun**, tel: (03) 353-8842, a few minutes from Yotsuya station, has an Irish landlord, good shepherd's pie and is open until midnight. **Pip's**, tel: (03) 470-0857, three minutes from Roppongi station, has electronic games as well as video and doesn't close until 6 a.m. -- by which time the trains are running again (the last ones at night are before 1 a.m.).

Tokyo's night scene: TOP topless show at a music hall, and BELOW Bosch-like faces in a Roppongi gay bar.

The city has numerous nightclubs, differing from those in the West mainly in the huge numbers of hostesses ready to greet you. They will fill your glass and empty your ashtray and may even murmur the odd sweet nothing but, be warned, not many of them are as sociable after hours as girls in other parts of Asia. A stylish club with topless dancers and French cuisine is Akasaka's **Cordon Bleu** tel: (03) 478-300; (03) 582-7800 after 6 p.m. Close to Akasaka-Mitsuke station; it's open until4 a.m. **Club Maiko** (tel: (03) 574-7745) in Ginza's Aster Building is open until midnight and offers a taste of old Kyoto, with dances performed by geisha and *maiko* (young apprentice geisha).

Things go on after dark in Tokyo that you wouldn't believe. There is, for example, the notorious club in the Shibuya section of town where the staple entertainment is live sex. The semi-nude lady performer tours the low circular stage offering the punters, mostly of student age, a dildo with which to do their worst to her, then later coaxes the drunker or more daring up on the stage to have sex. The only thing more astonishing than the frankness of the performance -- which has the eyes of old Bangkok hands popping -- is the atmosphere of innocence which prevails. Checking tickets at the entrance is a benign-looking old granny who lends this grim dive the air of a public bathhouse.

Tokyo's steamiest greeting awaits those who learn enough Japanese to read the word 'Soapland', plastered over scores of establishments as Shinjuku, Ikebukuro in the west and Senzoku in the east, the latter being the location of the famous 'nightless city', Yoshiwara, that flourished during the Edo period. Known as **Torako** until recently, these bath houses began to spring up in 1956 when the police closed down all the conventional cat houses, and the 20,000-odd masseuses who work in them nationwide have unique techniques for helping you to relax. They are hard to get into without Japanese company, and not cheap even then. The average fee for a bath and 'additional services' is about ¥25,000.

Taken together with love hotels, Turkish baths are now a 13-billion-dollar industry. If you and your girlfriend (or boyfriend) are fed up with paper-thin walls and lockless doors, a love hotel is the most discreet place you could retreat to. Many are masterpieces of pop architecture and one, the **Meguro Emperor**, closely modeled on a Bavarian castle, has become world-famous. There are no lobbies, no dining rooms, no registers. You rent a room for an hour or two at a time -- it's possible to stay the night but most people don't -- and pay about ¥5,000 for a couple of hours. But it's not just any old room; it may be equipped with wrap-around mirrors, video, S/M equipment... There are reckoned to be an incredible 35,000 love hotels throughout the country, soaking up a greater proportion of the GNP than is spent on defense. Access for foreign visitors is no problem.

After your love hotel you may like to cool off with a movie. A few little-known cinemas in the capital show movies all night, with a mixture of Japanese, American and European films. Some of the programs are excellent. Try **Theater Shinjuku** tel: (03) 352-1846 or **Theater Ikebukuro** tel: (03) 987-4311. programs at both start around 10 p.m. *Tokyo Journal* may be the only English language journal which carries useful listings of such movies.

Tokyo Night Tours
JTB and Gray Line run a number of night tours, introducing visitors to

some of the capital's special fun and games. Typically they start at 6 and finish around 11 p.m. and feature a *sukiyaki* dinner, a scene from the *kabuki* at the **Kabuki-za** or a nude show at Roppongi's **Kintaro** club and a geisha party. The geisha party is tailored to fit the imagined expectations of Western guests and may in consequence be a little weird. The rest, however, is lots of fun, and at least as real as the Kintaro's silicon-bolstered mammaries. Prices for the tours range between ¥9,000 without dinner and ¥13,000 with. Leaflets are available from the TIC.

Prices and other details of bars, discos and night spots can be found in the *Tokyo Journal* and *Tour Companion*. Tokyo is great in small doses, but after a while you will have the urge to escape. Where to go? The following are the most attractive and popular destinations within half a day's striking dis-

tance of the capital.

NIKKO

After spending some time in Tokyo's lowlands it is a source of joy and amazement to find that Japan is full of splendid mountains. One of the best places for enjoying them, and for seeing some of Japan's richest (and most uncharacteristic) architecture, is Nikko, about 140 km. (87 miles) north of the capital.

The chief attraction at Nikko is **Toshogu Shrine**, the gorgeous mausoleum of the mighty shogun Tokugawa Ieyasu, who died in 1616, and his grandson. But Nikko's history as a religious center goes back much further than that.

It is one of the centers of a curious cult called Mountain Buddhism. When Buddhism first arrived in the country about 1,500 years ago it mingled with certain native ascetic practices to produce a new cult whose devotees scaled mountains, lived as hermits and immersed themselves in icy water, all as a

OPPOSITE AND ABOVE Spectacular period costumes at Nikko's festival.

means of attaining spiritual enlightenment. Clad in white, these men and women still congregate at **Nantai-san**, the conical mountain at the heart of the Nikko region, in early August each year.

So Nikko was already famous when it was chosen 350 years ago as the site for Ieyasu's mausoleum.

Ieyasu was the first shogun of the Tokugawa line. It was he who, having united the country, fettered it so successfully that his heirs ruled for the next 250 years without serious challenge. The mausoleum was built to glorify his achievement, and all the apparatus and imagery of religion was harnessed to that cause.

It can be a confusing place for the visitor. For a start, it is totally unlike any other shrine or temple in the country. Most Japanese Buddhist temples are somber, even gloomy places, with structures of unpainted wood and little decoration. Shrines are often painted -- typically an orange-red color -- but usually in a simple manner. The gorgeous colors and overwhelming richness of decoration and carving at Nikko are unique in the country, and much more reminiscent of Chinese and Korean temples than of others in Japan. In fact, many of the craftsmen who worked on the shrine were of Korean stock.

The other respect in which Nikko is confusing is the carefree way it mixes elements of Buddhism and Shinto. The two religions are radically different (see **The Culture of Japan**), although early on they learned to live with each other. At Nikko, however , the most picturesque and impressive features of the architecture of the two religions are intermingled, not for religious reasons but to create an image of magnificence. The *torii* (gate) at the shrine's entrance, a Shinto feature, stands next to a Buddhist-style pagoda. Inside, but before the main gateway, stands a trough of water with wooden

ladles where visitors wash -- purify -- their hands and mouths, another Shinto feature. But the indescribably rich gateway itself is based on Buddhist models. And so on.

See how freely we control these gods and buddhas, the shogunate seems to be saying. How much more freely, then, do we control you, the people!

This secular orientation of the shrine is one of the reasons -- another being the large number of visitors -- for the lack of any strong religious atmosphere. Here are the roots of the secularism and materialism of modern Japan.

To put Nikko into perspective it is a good idea to visit one or two 'purer' temples and shrines elsewhere. Almost any of the temples in Kyoto or Kamakura will do, while the best shrine to visit is the most important one in the country, the bone-bare **Ise Jingu** (see **Kyoto** section).

For an instant contrast **Chuzenji Temple**, above Chuzenji Lake not far from the shrine, is recommended. The eighth-century statue of Kannon, goddess of mercy, enshrined there was carved from a living tree and practically glows with spirituality.

The lake is reached by one of the two hairpin Irohazaka Driveways, and the second is used for coming back down again. The scenery here is lovely, particularly in autumn. **Kegon Waterfall** near Chuzenji spa is also worth a visit, and if you have time take the lift down to the observatory at the bottom. The waterfall used to be a favorite spot for love suicides -- something the guides don't tell you.

If you're in Nikko and you're interested in pottery, why not make a side trip to the pottery town of **Mashiko** on the way back? This was for many years the home of Shoji Hamada, a great potter whose vigorous and simple work, decorated with a rapid technique that became his trademark, helped spread the fame of Japanese folk ceramics throughout the West. Hamada died a few years back, but his old farmhouse home is still there, as is his 'climbing kiln' (*noborigama*) -- a wood-fired clay kiln with several chambers built on a slope with the chimney at the top -- and a small museum of folk-art objects he collected on his travels.

Mashiko has been a pottery town for 150 years. Hamada moved there because of his admiration for the rough, folksy forms the town's potters produced , but he became so famous that, ironically enough, most of them are now producing rather uninspired imitations of *his* work. However, there are a few interesting potters among them, and some of the foreign potters based in the town do very fine work.

How To Get There
The quickest and cheapest way is by Tobu (private) line train from Asakusa station in Tokyo. Asakusa is the terminus of the Ginza subway line. The fastest train from Asakusa, the Tokkyu (special express) takes 1 hour 45 min-

utes, the Kaisoku (rapid) 2-1/2 hours.

Touring Nikko
Both the JTB and Fujita Travel service offer full-day tours from Tokyo to Nikko and back, departing at 8 a.m. from major hotels and returning at 7.30 p.m. Both visit the same places, including Toshogu Shrine and Lake Chuzenji. The JTB's, at ¥17,500 for adults, is ¥2,500 dearer but arguably more comfortable as the distance to Nikko is covered by a luxurious train rather than coach. Refreshments are available on the train. Both tours depart daily.

Two-day tours are also on offer, including one with a trip to Mashiko. Check with the TIC or any JTB office for details.

MT. FUJI
Every mountain in Japan is sacred according to the Shinto view of things. And Mt. Fuji (*Fuji-san*), the highest at over 3,776 meters (12,388 ft.) and the most beautiful, is the most sacred of all.

After weeks of cloud and rain, the skies over the capital clear and suddenly the mountain appears to the southwest, astonishingly high and sharply defined. Sometimes only the peak is visible, hanging in the air like the Cheshire Cat's smile. Towards dusk it is often the mountain's silhouette which dominates the skyline, black against the deepening blue of evening. No matter how many pictures one has seen of it, the volcano never loses its ability to startle and impress.

Before modern times it was frequently visible from Tokyo as the various place-names including the prefix Fujimi ('Fuji visible') attest. During the notoriously smoggy years of the 60s and early 70s, it disappeared almost entirely except for a few magical days in

OPPOSITE, The stupendous view from Hakone's ropeway.

autumn and winter, and although things have improved since then, and in really fine weather you can see it all the way from Narita Airport, it is best to get a little closer.

A trip round the **Fuji-go-ko (Fuji-Five-Lakes)** area in the national park at the mountain's base provides pleasant scenery and diversions such as boating and fishing, should the mountain decline to put in an appearance. For those determined to sit it out there are plenty of hotels and *ryokan*, but be warned that really clear days are rare except in autumn and winter.

Or you can climb the mountain. About 300,000 people do this every year, most of them during the open months of July and August. See **Off the Beaten Track** for details of how to set about it.

HAKONE

Mt. Fuji is the focus of an area, including the Fuji Five Lakes, the Izu Peninsula and Hakone, which might be called Tokyo's playground. The mighty, for-

ested flanks of the mountains and the pure waters of the lakes in this area have been spared the nastier intrusions of the modern world. Healing, sulfurous waters boil and bubble underground, spectacularly breaking the surface here and there and supplying the many inns and hotels with smelly but salubrious hot water.

Hakone, bordered by mountains and lying within the crater of an extinct volcano roughly 40 km. (25 miles) across, is the most accessible and perhaps the most rewarding area for the visitor. Tokyo lacks gardens: Hakone is the compensation, paid in one splendid lump sum. Only 1-1/2 hours from the capital by express, half that by Shinkansen, it is the perfect place to relax and replenish your oxygen supply.

Gateway to the area is **Odawara**. Here you can leave your gleaming 'bullet' and board a smart little train from another era on the Hakone Tozan line which will haul you up with many a switchback into the heart of the mountains. You will pass through several intriguing villages full of hot spa

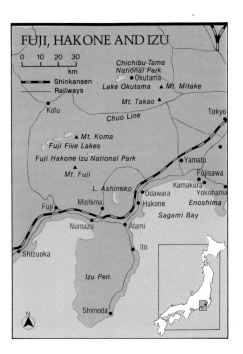

FUJI, HAKONE AND IZU

hotels, but the first imperative stop is **Chokoku-no-Mori**. This means 'Woods of Sculpture' and is the name of the magnificent open-air sculpture museum which borders the railway line. Admission is expensive at ¥1,000 (¥1,300 including the new Picasso Hall) per adult but it's worth it. The works of art, including several very famous pieces by Moore, Hepworth and others, are imaginatively displayed against the lush backdrop of the mountains. With diversions for children and plenty to eat and drink, boredom is impossible.

Getting back on the train and going to the end of the line you change to a cable-car which carries you even higher to aptly named **Owakudani**, the 'Valley of Greater Boiling'. A foul stench of hydrogen sulfide fills the air. Vivid yellow gashes mark the places where the steam belches from the earth. And in one or two small pools strange gray material is indeed boiling away with great frenzy. It's all very impressive and is said to be the only place of its type in Japan. Hot water from

Owakudani is piped to hot spas for miles around.

One of the finest views of Mt. Fuji -- should it be visible at all, of course -- is from the ropeway which swings you down the steep mountainside from Owakudani to **Lake Ashinoko**. Having arrived there you can continue this carnival of transportation by crossing the lake on what is claimed to be a replica of a seventeenth-century English man-of-war, 'modeled after the baroque manner as percise (*sic*) as possible'.

The Tokaido, the old road which led from Edo (Tokyo) to Kyoto and Osaka, passed through Hakone. Near where the ferry docks at Hakone-machi is the old **Barrier Guardhouse** where travelers in pre-modern days were searched and their documents rigorously checked. The guardhouse has been reconstructed in the original style and contains life-size models of travelers and guards. In a nearby museum, mystifyingly described as **Hakone Materials**

OPPOSITE AND ABOVE The craft on Hakone's Lake Ashinoko.

Hall, are many old relics from those days.

And if you want a taste of what transportation was like way back then, the course of the old road has been preserved for several miles east of the Barrier Guardhouse. Narrow, winding and precipitous, though paved for much of the distance with large stones, it inspires respect for the messengers of those days who, clad in loin cloths and straw sandals, dashed across the country along roads like this.

These are some of the activities Hakone offers. Others include camping, skating -- at the peak of **Mt. Koma**, the area's central peak -- and golf. For more ideas and detailed information see the TIC's mini-guide to the area.

How To Get There

Take the Tokaido Shinkansen from Tokyo station to Odawara. It covers the 83.9 km. (52.1 miles) distance in 42 minutes. Alternatively, the Odakyu (private) line's luxurious Romance Car train runs between Shinjuku in Tokyo and Yumoto in Hakone, via Odawara, in 75 minutes.

KAMAKURA

Tourists usually stop in Kamakura, a seaside town about one hour south of Tokyo, to see the **Dai-butsu** (Great Buddha). This is a good reason, for the 11.4 meter (37 ft.) high bronze figure is strikingly beautiful, but there are many reasons for prolonging the visit beyond the customary half hour.

For one thing, Kamakura is the nearest really attractive town to Tokyo. Enclosed on three sides by small but steep and densely wooded hills, and on the fourth by the sea, its atmosphere is much older than Tokyo's, while its air is much fresher.

The hills and the sea made it marvelously easy to defend in the Middle

Ages and this is why the first shogun, Minamoto Yoritomo chose to raise it from a humble fishing village to capital of the country when he seized control in 1192. The Great Buddha was one of the greatest products of the Kamakura period which ensued, but there are many others.

In the middle of the town, ten minutes from the station at the far end of an avenue of cherry trees, is the magnificent **Hachiman Shrine**, devoted to the god of war and built by Yoritomo in gratitude for his victory. Among the votary creatures kept in the shrine's grounds is a flock of doves.

Not long after Yoritomo's rule began, Zen Buddhism was introduced from China, and several fine old temples of the Rinzai Zen sect are tucked away in the hills around the town. Best for atmosphere, perhaps, are **Engakuji**, opposite Kita-Kamakura station, and **Kenochoji,** ten minutes from Engakuji on the road to the city centre. In particular Engakuji's tall trees,

shady paths and soulful old buildings reverberate with the somber spirituality of the Kamakura period.

Several well-marked and well-tramped hiking courses follow the ridges of the town's hills. The **Daibutsu** course, for example, goes from near Kita-Kamakura station to a spot near the Great Buddha. It's about an hour's pleasant stroll from end to end . On the way, you can drop in at **Zeni-Arai Benten**, a very popular shrine, to wash your money. It should double in value -- sometime.

And finally, what about the Great Buddha? It is a remarkable piece of work. Cast in bronze in 1252 it has survived the storms, typhoons and earthquakes which destroyed the temple building that used to enclose it. The rock-solid posture and the sublime calm of the face successfully embody the ideals of Buddhism.

Kamakura has a lighter side, too -- the seaside, where Tokyoites flock in their thousands every summer weekend to swim, sail, windsurf and sunbathe. The lack of alternatives helps them to ignore the quantities of garbage that are continually washed up on the beach. Foreign visitors do not always find it so easy.

Along the scenic coast between Kamakura and the nearby city of Fujisawa runs the single-track Enoden railway line. Some 15 minutes from Kamakura it stops at **Enoshima**, and ten minutes' walk away is the holy island of that name, reached by a bridge. It's small, steep and notably overdeveloped, but the shrines and tower at the top of the island are popular. If your legs ache by the time you reach the shrine precincts you can, for a small sum, take an escalator to the top.

How To Get There

Japan National Railways' Yokosuka (pronounced '*Yokos'ka*') line covers the distance from Tokyo to Kamakura in just over an hour. The platform at Tokyo is underground, on the Marunouchi side of the station.

If you wind up your visit in Enoshima, there are two other ways of getting back to Tokyo.

The private Odakyu line runs between Odakyu Enoshima station and Shinjuku, in the heart of Tokyo. The fastest trains (*Tokkyu*, special express), which run roughly once an hour, cover the distance in 1 hour 10 minutes. Like most private lines, the Odakyu line is much cheaper, and consequently more crowded, than JNR.

Alternatively, you can take an exhilarating 13-minute ride on the monorail that swoops and climbs through the hills between Enoshima and Ofuna, and catch JNR's Tokaido line to Yokohama and Tokyo from there.

At Kamakura's Hachiman Shrine OPPOSITE a diminutive but elegant subsidiary shrine and RIGHT wooden tablets bearing the names of the shrine's benefactors.

Touring Hakone and Kamakura

Both the JTB and Fujita Travel Service have full-day tours that take in the most famous attractions of Hakone, plus the Great Buddha at Kamakura. Both depart from Tokyo's major hotels at 8 a.m., and the fare for both is ¥17,500 for adults. Both tours involve visits to the Great Buddha, Owakudani and a lake cruise, and both return to Tokyo by Shinkansen train.

NAGOYA

The fastest Tokaido Shinkansen train, the Hikari, stops only once between Tokyo and Kyoto: at Nagoya. The two million- plus people who live and work in this city's remarkably wide, clean and carefully planned streets constitute Japan's fifth largest urban population. It is not known as a center for tourism, and even native Nagoyans are hard put to name their city's charms. But it is a major business and conference center, and if you have cause to visit you will find a variety of ways to while away the time.

Nagoya is also the gateway to two of Japan's most worthwhile sightseeing areas: Ise and Toba to the south, and the Hida area, including the city of Takayama, to the north.

Nagoya's History

In the seventeenth century the great shogun Tokugawa Ieyasu built a major castle where Nagoya Castle now stands, and as so often happened in Japan, a city grew up around its skirts. Crafts which had been practiced in the area since ancient times -- especially pottery -- flourished, and the city became a major cultural center.

Nearly all vestiges of this were unfortunately destroyed in the war, but the people of Nagoya took advantage of the disaster to rebuild the city on a grid plan. In 1959 they also rebuilt the castle, prudently in ferro-concrete. The old trades -- porcelain, *cloisonné* and textiles -- flourished again, but were overtaken in importance by modern heavy and chemical industries: iron and steel, automobiles, ship-building, plastics, fertilizers, drugs. Ideally located on the Pacific and in the center of the great Tokaido industrial belt, well-watered Nagoya is one of the modern world's most massive and smoothly turning dynamos.

Seeing the City

The **Kanko Annaisho** -- the Tourist Information Office (not to be confused with the TIC) -- is on the east side of Nagoya station. The people there are helpful and have useful English-language leaflets. City sightseeing bus tours are conducted in Japanese but are a good way of getting acquainted with the city quickly. There are several every day, the earliest leaving at 9.30 a.m.

Winter in Nagoya: OPPOSITE a temple in the city and RIGHT a section of the castle wall.

The castle is the high-point of most tours. Although the main building is less than 25 years old, it is a faithful copy of the original (unlike Osaka Castle, for example, which is smaller than its model) and some of the gates and turrets around it have survived from the seventeenth century. It's a little too obvious that it is made of concrete, but the lift which whisks visitors to the fifth floor will be appreciated by anybody who has trudged up the hundreds of steps in a genuine

Japanese castle.

On the way down, in the well-lit exhibition spaces, there are weapons, armour, painted screens and, on the fourth floor, cases of beautiful paper dolls representing the city's October parade of feudal lords. Entrance costs ¥300, for which you also get an informative and well-written leaflet.

Atsuta Shrine, the most important in the city, is one of the oldest in the country and draws streams of pilgrims. Its buildings are reminiscent of those at Ise (see below, **Kyoto and Points West**).

Nagoya's city center, **Sakae**, is dominated by the 180 meter (590 ft.) high TV tower, and the park-cum-boulevard in which the tower stands is remarkably spacious.

Through no fault of its own Nagoya is miserably short of old buildings, but a 60-minute bus ride away from the city center is a treasure house of Japanese architectural history. Called **Meiji Mura**, it is the highlight of one of the regular daily bus tours.

Unique in Japan, the large hillside park is home for more than 50 of the most significant buildings of the Meiji period (1868-1912). Like all such parks it rates nil for atmosphere, but as a series of vivid demonstrations of the way the Japanese variously imitated, adapted and resisted Western architectural styles, it is unbeatable. Among the attractions are a prison, a bathhouse, a small *kabuki* theater and the house occupied in turn by the novelists Mori Ogai and Natsume Soseki.

Back in the city, but not included in any of the regular tours, is the model factory of **Noritake**, Nagoya's famous porcelain firm. *Kanko Annaisho* -- Tourist Information Office will help arrange your visit.

Due to the city's grid plan, finding your way around is straightforward, and the subway system is easy to use. (It may also be the only one in the world with curtains.) Ask at the Tourist Information Office for a map.

The subway will take you as far as **Nagoyako**, Japan's third largest port, where some of the vast number of Japanese cars which are for sale overseas will probably be lined up for your inspection.

Nagoya at Night

Sakae, two subway stops from Nagoya station, is the place to go for evening entertainment. Due to its wide streets and four-square architecture, Sakae has neither the style of Tokyo's Roppongi nor the cheerful garishness of

Dottonbori in Osaka. There is, however, plenty going on.

An invaluable guide to straight entertainment -- theater, movies, concerts -- as well as daytime events is the monthly English-language *Nagoya Calendar*, published by Nagoya City Hall. If you can't get a copy at the Tourist Information Office, call the City Hall's liaison and protocol Division tel: (052) 951-1814 and ask about it.

The only guide to the less formal night-life, however, is your own nose. There are many restaurants, bars, 'snacks' and cabarets to try. Nagoya's only culinary speciality is *kishimen*, wide, flat wheat noodles in broth, but excellent food of all sorts is available.

One particular shop deserves special mention. This is **Gomitori**, a *nomi-ya* (bar) in the heart of town which serves an amazing selection of exotic delicacies at reasonable prices in rooms charmingly decked out with Japanese antiques. Specialities of the house include horsemeat *sashimi*, loaches, frogs (in season), spare ribs, *natto* (fermented soybeans), turtle soup and *kushiyaki* (skewered, barbecued pieces of chicken, etc.). There are two branches, one close by Nagoya Kanko Hotel. For directions, phone (052) 241-0041 (in Japanese).

How To Get There

It's not difficult. Nagoya is 2 hours from Tokyo, 50 minutes from Kyoto and 1 hour 7 minutes from Osaka by the Tokaido Shinkansen's fastest train, the Hikari. All Tokaido Shinkansen trains stop at Nagoya.

Touring Nagoya

The Japanese-language city bus tours were mentioned above. There are no scheduled tours of the city conducted in English.

Nagoya is one of the best places to begin (or end) trips to the holy shrines of Ise and the seaside area of Toba (to the southwest) and to the well-preserved villages of Tsumago, Magome and Narai and the elegant city of Takayama to the northeast. For details of the former, see the end of the **Kyoto** section. The latter places are described in **Off the Beaten Track**.

Nagoya is also close (40 minutes by train) to the old city of **Gifu**. No longer very picturesque (blame the bombs), Gifu is nonetheless a center of picturesque trades -- parasol and lantern making. It is also, more significantly, the center of the ancient sport of *ukai*, or cormorant fishing.

Every summer night (except when there is a full moon) fishing boats prowl up the Nagaragawa River at Gifu. Suspended from the prow of each is a fiery torch; and each boat also contains a number of cormorants on leads. lured by the light, *ayu* (delicious sweetfish) rise to the surface, where the cormorants snap them up and bear them to the boats. This very ancient ritual takes place under the eyes of hundreds of spectators, almost all of them river-borne too, and most of them enjoying snacks or full-blown picnics washed down with quantities of sake. For some ¥2,200 (May, September, October) ¥2,400 (June, July, August) (exclusive of food and drink) you could be one of them. Reservations can be made at JTB offices or in Gifu on the day.

KYOTO AND POINTS WEST

The Kansai district, which includes the nation's second largest city, Osaka, as well as the old capitals of Kyoto and Nara, is where the Japanese became Japanese: where they first put down

OPPOSITE A Nagoya mother and child in their New Year holiday finery.

113

roots, built cities and started to decide who they were. Five hundred kilometers from Tokyo, it is the old heartland and still Tokyo's greatest rival.

Osaka's fame has long rested on commerce. 'Are you making any money?' was the customary greeting between the merchants in the old days, and financial sharpness is still the Osaka stereotype in other parts of the country.

KYOTO

Kyoto is only 30 minutes from Osaka by the fastest train, but the dialect, *Kyoto-ben*, is quite different -- and it's one of many profound differences between the two cities. People elsewhere in Japan say that when a woman speaks *Kyoto-ben* it sounds like poetry, but when a man speaks it it makes you squirm, and this is indicative, too. Kyoto is one of the most feminine of places and contrasts starkly with the rough practicality of Osaka down the track.

Kyoto is also the one place in Japan you should visit, even if you go nowhere else. Capital of the country for more than a thousand years, it is the cradle of almost everything that is uniquely Japanese, and though designed along Chinese lines it is the place where the medieval Japanese first shook off that tradition and started to go their own way. As the only Japanese city of substance to escape wartime bombing -- at the plea, it is said, of a highly placed American Japanophile -- a great deal of this ancient beauty survives: in temples, shrines, palaces, castles, aristocratic villas... There are also theaters, craft workshops and museums, geisha houses -- and beautiful women. The young women of Kyoto do full justice to their surroundings.

You can 'do' Kyoto in a day or less, but you should stay longer if you can. It is an elusive city, and with its modern

steel and ferro-concrete and snarled-up traffic it doesn't at first seem anything out of the ordinary. Much of the charm is on a delicate scale: give yourself time to drop in to that little temple you would otherwise march right past, to get lost in the geisha district, to follow the winding course of a city stream. There are no grand European-style prospects in the city, and the view from the 131-meter (430 ft.) Kyoto Tower outside the station (the proprietors claim it harmonizes well with classical Kyoto) is banal in the extreme. You have to get close to the city and become a part of the picture before you can start to relish it.

Kyoto's History

Kyoto was founded in 794 as the capital of Japan. Like nearby Nara, the capital for the preceding 70-odd years,

to Tokyo in 1869 might have been a final disaster but the city survived, its old trades shored up by modern industries. The atmosphere of the city remains as refined and aristocratic -- snobbish, many Japanese say -- as ever. The enthronement ceremonies for new emperors still take place there.

Seeing the City

First stop for all visitors who wish to explore Kyoto is the TIC on the ground floor of the Kyoto Tower Building, two minutes' waik from the main station (north exit). The busy but friendly and very helpful staff will give you a map, an explanatory pamphlet and any other help or advice you require. Brochures describing city tours are freely available and there are notices advertising upcoming concerts, plays and festivals.

The center is open from 9 a.m. to 5 p.m. on weekdays and 9 a.m. to noon on Saturdays. It's closed on Sundays and national holidays.

Armed with your map, you are ready to set out. Here are some of the places you should see.

Temples

Kyoto has an amazing number of temples -- some 1,500. Many of the most charming are located around the city's edges where they enjoy the serenity of the encircling mountains. The first one you will encounter when you start walking, however, is slap bang in the middle of town, **Higashi Honganji**, the city's largest wooden building. The victim of many fires, it was most recently rebuilt in 1895. Most of the temple's buildings are closed to the public, so content yourself with an 'ooh' and an 'ah' and pass on.

it was designed according to Chinese concepts, with nine broad streets running from east to west, intersected by a number of avenues running from south to north. This street plan persists to the present day and makes the city a blessedly easy place to get about in.

Heian-kyo -- 'Capital of Peace' -- was one of its early names, and its golden age was the Heian period, from its foundation to the twelfth century. During these years the imperial court lived in great splendor and the city's artisans developed the skills necessary to satisfy the courtiers' luxurious tastes. These were the centuries when Kyoto was the country's true capital.

In the twelfth century, power was wrested from the court by military leaders based near present-day Tokyo, and the city began a long and gentle decline. The transfer of emperor and court

---

OPPOSITE AND ABOVE Elements of Kyoto's ancient cityscape including TOP the huge Heian Shrine crowded with New Year visitors.

One of the first things you will see when you get through customs at Narita Airport is a large poster showing the roof of a pagoda silhouetted against an uncannily orange evening sky. This is the famous pagoda of **Kiyomizu Temple**, one of the city's most splendid. Its verandah projects over a cliff and is supported by 139 meter (456 ft.) high wooden columns: vertigo is assured.

The temple is on the east of the city, a stiff ten-minute walk from Kiyomizu-michi bus stop up through the narrow streets where much of Kyoto's characteristic pottery is produced and sold. The temple was founded in 798 but re-erected in 1633. The verandah is a miracle of wooden engineering and offers great views of the city.

Keeping close to the hills and moving north a little, we reach **Nanzenji Temple**. The easiest access is from Keage station on the Keishin line. This enormous temple, which contains 12 subordinate temples, is noted for its *fusuma* (sliding door) paintings and its exquisite gardens. It is a Zen temple, headquarters of the Nanzenji school of the Rinzai sect.

In the grounds there is a curious red-brick Victorian aqueduct. Following this to the end we find that its only function is to feed the little waterfall which is the main feature of one of the gardens. From the place where the garden is designed to be admired, the aqueduct is, of course, invisible.

The road leading to Nanzenji is lined with restaurants which specialize in *yudofu*, literally 'tofu with hot water', though the reality is a bit more interesting than that. Still, prices are high for what is basically a simple dish, fancily presented.

Daitokuji Temple in the north of the city (Daitokuji-mae station) is another enormous Rinzai Zen establishment with numerous subsidiary temples. Pretty gardens and artworks of great age

and beauty abound. Some of the sub-temples are open to the public, but an entrance fee must be paid for each one. It is generally worth it: they are full of charming surprises.

In the grounds of the temple there is also a restaurant which specializes in Kyoto's vegetarian cuisine. It does not look like a restaurant so much as another temple, and the atmosphere is appropriately hushed and meditative. The food is, needless to say, very pretty. Go with a friend -- ideally a Japanese one.

West of Daitokuji is the famous **Kinkakuji**, the 'Temple of the Golden

Mellow beauty of Kyoto in OPPOSITE Chionin Temple garden, ABOVE, TOP the famous rock garden of Ryoanji Temple and BELOW the garden of Heian Shrine.

Pavilion' in Yukio Mishima's novel of the same name (Kinkakuji-mae station, one stop west of Daitokuji-mae). The pavilion of this temple, situated on a small lake, has two claims to fame aside from its extraordinary beauty: its walls are entirely covered in gold leaf, and it was burnt to the ground by a deranged priest (the hero of Mishima's novel) in 1950. It was rebuilt exactly as before -- and not, for once, in ferroconcrete -- in 1955.

A couple of kilometers from Kinka kuji to the southwest is **Ryoanji Temple** (no convenient railway station). This temple's austere and simple stone garden, composed of a few mossy rocks arranged in a sea of gravel which is carefully raked into place daily, is the most famous of its kind in Japan. Yet 'garden' seems the wrong word for it: apart from the moss, nothing grows here at all.

Ryoanji's fame, which has gone round the world, has perhaps been counterproductive. People who have read ecstatic descriptions of the garden and its metaphysical meaning arrive burdened with grand ideas and expectations and often go away disappointed, because the garden is very simple. Happy is the visitor who, knowing nothing about it beforehand, arrives and dangles his legs over the verandah -- and, looking at his watch, finds that an hour has slipped by since he started gazing at it. Words maul a place like this.

Unfortunately, this type of experience is almost impossible due to the loudspeaker which babbles on all day about the garden's tranquillity. Arrive early in the morning -- before 9 -- to avoid this. The temple will not be officially open but a monk should let you in.

Back in the center of town, about a kilometer east of Kyoto station, is a remarkable temple known as **San-jusangendo**, which glitters with the reflected light of a thousand and one small images of Kannon, the goddess of mercy. The tall 'thousand-handed' image of Kannon around which they cluster was carved in 1254. The temple is a great favorite with visitors.

Shrines

Kyoto is dotted with shrines, though they are not nearly as numerous as temples. As elsewhere in Japan they are distinguishable from temples by the *torii* (gate) which invariably marks the entrance to the sacred ground. This is often painted red, as are the shrine's buildings.

Suspended outside the shrine's main hall is a bell which makes a dry rattling noise when shaken by means of a rope which hangs below it. This is one way of arousing the attention of the enshrined deity before praying -- another is clapping your hands.

Kyoto's most impressive shrine, though not the oldest, is **Heian Jingu**. This monumental piece of work was built in 1895 to commemorate the 1,100th anniversary of the city's foundation, and every year it is the locus for the city's **Jidai Matsuri** (Festival of the Ages), a historical costume parade on a grand scale (see the **Festivals** section of **The Culture of Japan** for details).

Despite its enormous proportions, Heian Jingu is in fact a smaller replica of a much older shrine, built in 794. It's within walking distance of Nanzenji Temple.

An older and more restrained and soulful shrine is **Kitano**, a short distance east of Ryoanji Temple. Others are scattered around the city, charming but not worthy of special mention. Note how local children use the precincts of shrines as playgrounds: this is one of Shinto's public functions. The public park is a modern idea imported from the West.

Palaces

Kyoto's **Old Imperial Palace (Kyoto Gosho)**, which covers a large area in the centre of the city, was the emperor's home before he packed his bags and moved to Tokyo. Getting to see it is something of a hassle: you must visit the offices of the Imperial Household Agency located there, fill in an application form, show your passport and wait for a short while. You are, after all, in the presence of the ghosts of many emperors and the

San-In main line, was the home of the great shogun Ieyasu whenever he was in Kyoto and is the best place to get a glimpse of his luxurious (and highly security-conscious) lifestyle. The castle, designed as a lavish habitat rather than a fortress, is crammed with invaluable works of art and craft, including carvings, paintings, metal work and furniture.

The single most famous feature of the castle is the *uguisubari*, the 'bush warbler floor' of the corridor in the first

descendants of the sun goddess!

At the same time you can apply for permission to visit one of Kyoto's architectural musts, the **Katsura Rikyu mansion**. Say you hope to see it a day or two later and the imperial bureaucrats will usually consent.

If you take a Japanese friend with you to the palace he will have to wait outside: only foreigners are allowed such easy access. Japanese have to wait months for permission and many are turned down flat.

Nijo Castle, near Nijo station on the

building, which warbles under the lightest tread. This was to warn guards that an intruder -- perhaps a would-be assassin -- was on the premises.

The castle is surrounded by a pleasant garden but the trees in it are new: in the old days there were none. The sight of falling leaves was said to be too depressing for the resident samurai.

LEFT Dressed up for a visit to a shrine. At Heian Shrine RIGHT children play by the fountain.

If you go to the trouble of getting permission to visit Katsura Rikyu, you won't regret it. According to many it is the crowning glory of Japanese domestic architecture.

In Japanese the adopted word '*manshon*' means a block of flats. Katsura Rikyu, however, is a mansion in the old English sense -- a country pile. But it has none of the grandiloquence or pomposity of Western equivalents. With its clean lines and masterly proportions, it is almost a modern building,

are they faring elsewhere?

Arts and Crafts

Many cities, towns and villages in Japan boast of one particular craft which has been practiced in that place for generations and cannot be found in exactly the same form anywhere else. Kyoto, however, has not one craft but a whole spectrum, including silk weaving, dyeing, embroidery, pottery, lacquer ware, *cloisonné*, woodblock prints, bamboo ware and others.

except that the quality of the craftsmanship which greets the eye at every turn is beyond the dreams of any modern architect.

In the spring of 1982 the building was reopened to the public after six years of work, during which it was reconstructed from scratch. The fact that it was possible to reproduce the seventeenth-century craftsmanship of the original to the same high standards speaks volumes for the strength of Japanese craft traditions.

And what of those traditions? How

Some of these -- silk weaving, for example -- date back to the foundation of the city in the eighth century. Some -- again, with weaving and dyeing are examples -- have developed into modern industrialized concerns with an annual output worth hundreds of millions of dollars. But even in these cases the traditional craft techniques are maintained as a relatively small but vital part of the industry.

Other crafts such as lacquer and bamboo ware are quite resistant to radical modernization, but their fame

120

within Japan allows the craftsmen to ask high enough prices to keep going.

Craft is a fascinating as well as a vital aspect of the city's life, and there are a number of opportunities for visitors to learn more about them. Here are some of the most interesting:

The **Kyoto Handicrafts Center** is a ten-minute walk due north from Higashiyama-Sanjo station. Dropping in here is the single most convenient way to see craftsmen at work, weavers, potters and woodblock makers among them. A good selection of their products is on sale as well.

The area of steep, narrow streets leading up to **Kiyomizu Temple** is Kyoto's well-known pottery-producing area, and potters can be seen at work in several of the shops here. One of the greatest of them lived in this neighborhood. His name was Kanjiro Kawai and his house is open to the public. Here you can inspect his work and the traditional 'climbing kiln' in which he fired it.

Two hundred meters east of Nishi-Kyogoku station is **Kyoto Yuzen Cultural Hall**, and here you can observe the traditional method of silk-dyeing in progress -- although *painting* gives a closer idea of how the craft looks in action. This is how they make the material for those gorgeous kimonos you see around town. Enjoy the serenity of the atmosphere in the workshop: pure Kyoto.

As well as these live attractions there are a number of museums which specialize in crafts of various sorts:

Kyoto Center of Traditional Industry (Dento Sanyo Kaikan). This museum has a great collection of traditional craft products as well as a reproduction of a traditional Kyoto house. It's to the right of the **National Museum of Modern Art** near Higashiyama Sanjo station.

Costume Museum. Located near Nishi-Honganji station, this museum charts the ways in which Japanese costume has changed over the past 2,000 years.

Other museums likely to prove of interest are:

Kiyotaki Folkcraft Museum
Kyoto Ceramic Hall
Kyoto Folkcraft Museum
Kodai Yuzen

For details of all these contract the TIC.

Kyoto At Night
Kyoto may not boogie like Tokyo but it has some suave steps of its own. It's

OPPOSITE Kyoto artisans at work: LEFT a carver of Noh masks and RIGHT a maker of *geta*, Japanese-style clogs, ABOVE: The bright, inviting clutter of a Kyoto sidestreet.

one of the few Japanese cities within where in the early evening the citizens do the Mediterranean thing and stroll along the streets, at least during the warmer months. Join them: it's a pleasant way to get to know the city at night.

Drift around the **Gion** section on the east bank of the Kamo River, admire the quiet elegance of the old townhouses there, in a number of which geisha still live and work. Cross the bridge at the **Minamiza Theater**, home of Kyoto's *kabuki*, back to the west bank, then turn right up the narrow street closest to the river and parallel to it running north. This is **Ponto-cho** and it's the heart of the city's amusement quarter. Many bars and restaurants line the street, some forbiddingly traditional or expensive (remember to check before ordering), others welcoming and relatively cheap. The ones on the right look out over the river: there you can feel cool, even in summer.

There are plenty of other ways to pass the time: first-rate cinemas, *kabuki* and *noh* plays, coffee shops specializing in Beatles records or jazz (some people call Kyoto the jazz capital of the world).

Back on the east bank of the river is **Gion Corner** (also known as **Gion Kaburenjo Theater**) where you can catch one of the twice-nightly presentations of traditional arts and drama. The tea ceremony, flower-arrangement and *bunraku* puppet plays are among the arts demonstrated -- and a handier way to sample traditional Japanese culture has not been devised.

One bridge north, in the Sanjo area, is the **Bel-ami**, Kyoto's most famous nightclub, with a first-rate floor show and dancing every night.

Shopping

Kyoto is the best place to buy locally made craft products. A map available at the TIC, the 'Shopping Guide Map of Kyoto' shows where. For general shopping Kyoto has a number of excellent department stores.

How To Get There

The simplest and most popular way is by Tokaido Shinkansen from Tokyo Station. The Hikari, which stops at only one station on the way (Nagoya), covers the 513 km. (319 miles) in 2 hours 53 minutes, while the Kodama takes 3 hours 53 minutes.

For those on a tight budget, JNR operates a convenient night bus, leaving the Yaesu side of Tokyo station at 11 p.m. and arriving at Kyoto station at 7.45 a.m. When the bus is not crowded it's possible to sleep fairly soundly in the reclining seats.

Alternatively, you can fly to Kyoto, either from within the country or from overseas, landing at Osaka's international airport. Frequent buses ply between the airport and Kyoto's major hotels.

Touring Kyoto

Once you've arrived, several lightning tours are available to give you a taste of the city.

Fujita Travel Service's **Good Morning Tour** visits Nijo Castle, the Imperial Palace (Nishijin Textile Centre on Sundays and holidays), Kinkakuji and the Kyoto Handicraft Center. Departing from major city hotels between 8.20 and 9 a.m. it returns at noon. The adult fare is ¥4,300.

Both Fujita and JTB offer afternoon tours calling at Heian Jingu, Sanjusangendo and Kiyomizu Temple. The adult fare is ¥4,300. In the case of Fujita you can stitch morning and afternoon tours together to make a full-day tour.

The JTB also offers a **Kyoto Garden Tour**, which for ¥5,000 takes visitors round three celebrated gardens, including the rock garden at Ryoanji, in an afternoon.

See Kyoto TIC for leaflets giving details of all these tours.

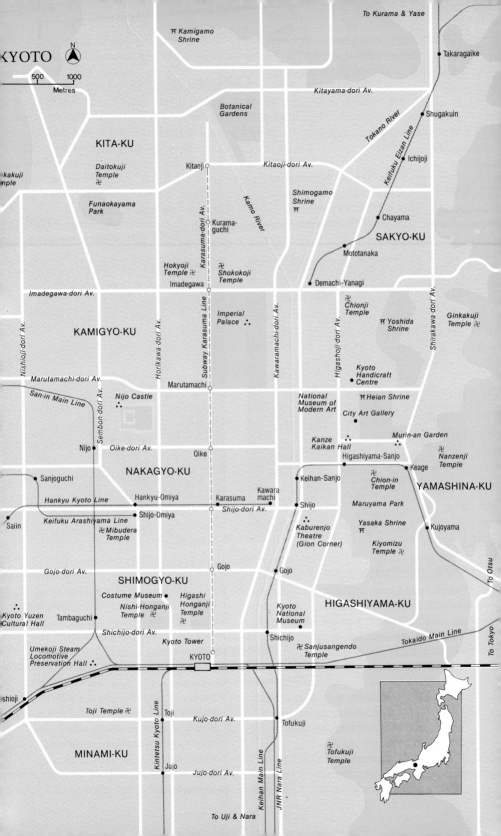

Other tours with trips to Nara, including those originating in Tokyo, are described at the end of the **Nara** section below.

Kyoto is the perfect base for making excursions to other places of interest in the Kansai district. Foremost of these is Nara.

NARA

Kyoto was not the first city the Japanese built under the inspiration of China. That honor goes to Nara.

Before Chinese influence began to surge into the country, and while administration was still a simple matter, it was the custom for each new emperor to choose a new capital. In 710, however, the empress regnant decided to pitch camp for good: a city was laid out -- though never more than partially constructed -- along rectangular Chinese lines, and although it only lasted 74 years those years encompassed the reigns of seven successive emperors.

In 784 the capital was transferred to the southwest of present-day Kyoto and Nara's tide began to recede. The pro-

cess has been going on ever since. Of Japan's old capitals, Kyoto is still thriving in its own quiet way, while the population of Kamakura is almost exactly the same as it was in the thirteenth century. Nara alone has slipped, and is now a grassy ghost town. Many of the temples and shrines are still standing, but the courtiers and common people, the servants and warriors and worshipers have all vanished. Only tame deer and tourists remain.

It's great place to visit, if only for a day. Setting off from Kyoto in the

morning -- a very pleasant 50-minute ride on the luxurious private Kinki Nippon line train -- you can see most of what should be seen and return, sated but happy, in the evening. Alternatively, you can put yourself in the hands of the JTB or Fujita Travel Service, both of which run afternoon Nara tours (and the JTB a full-day one too) from Kyoto hotels. See the end of this section for details.

(As a passenger on the Kinki Nippon train you are by definition a Kinki Nippon Tourist. If you want to explain the joke to a Japanese friend, have a good dictionary handy and be prepared for a long haul. He or she will then explain patiently that 'Kinki' means the Kyoto/Nara/Osaka area.)

Several, though not all, of Nara's attractions are located in **Nara Park** which is close to the station. Really nice parks are unusual in Japan so enjoy this excellent specimen to the full. If you plan a picnic, however, bring enough for the deer, which are harmless but always hungry.

As Nara was the first city to be established under Chinese influence, it is not surprising that it was also the first place in Japan where Buddhism flourished. This was very much a state-sponsored affair with imperial magnificence clearly in view. The temples are large, dignified and purely Chinese in style -- in fact, they are the best surviving examples anywhere of the architecture of China's T'ang dynasty. The ones on the continent were destroyed during the Mongol invasions.

Typical of the Chinese style -- although the present building is a later reconstruction -- is Nara's biggest attraction, **Todaiji**, the world's largest wooden building, containing the world's largest bronze figure, the Great Buddha.

This Buddha is 16.2 meters (53.1 ft.) high, compared with the 11.4 meters (37.4 ft.) of the Great Buddha in Kamakura. It is certainly impressive, and somehow the temple's gloom makes it seem even huger than it is. It has had an unhappy history, however -- decapitated in earthquakes, partially melted in fires and patched together numerous times -- and these accidents have left the statue with a slightly offputting Frankenstein monster quality.

The JTB's official guide tells us that the image is 'worshipped with the utmost reverence'. This may be so, but the sect which focused on the image disappeared centuries ago. The sea of popular devotion has long since retreated, leaving monuments like this

sticking up like rocks out of the sand.

Kofukuji Temple is another of Nara's great landmarks, famous for its two pagodas, one five- and one three-story. It was founded by a member of the most powerful court family. After a period of decline during which it moved twice its name was shrewdly changed to Kofukuji which means 'Happiness-Producing Temple'. Result: instant popularity.

Kasuga Shrine is hidden away deep in the woods in the east of Nara Park

and is a place to experience the tranquillity of Shinto: you can almost smell the sanctity. **Ise Jingu**, Shinto's most important shrine, (see below) has this quality to an even stronger degree. Like Ise, Kasuga used to be reconstructed regularly every 20 years. The custom continues at Ise but has apparently lapsed here.

OPPOSITE AND ABOVE Nara's air of antiquity encompasses both the buildings, KASUGA SHRINE, OPPOSITE PAGE LEFT, and the people.

There are 3,000 lanterns at Kasuga and they are lighted twice a year. See the **Festivals** section of **The Culture of Japan** for details.

Around Nara

Byodoin Temple is also known as **Phoenix Temple**: the hall was originally designed to represent the Japanese equivalent of that mythical bird descending to earth. Marvel at the lightness and elegance of these eleventh-century buildings, which are genuinely bird-like.

Horyuji, the single most worthwhile spot in the Nara area, is also about the hardest to get to -- although no harder than hopping on and off a bus, which goes from Nara-Kintetsu (Kinki Nippon) station. Note that none of the regular tours visit this beautiful and seminal temple.

When you get off the bus you will find you are out in the country, though presumably it was part of the capital in its heyday. A short walk will bring you to **Horyuji**, one of the first Buddhist temples in Japan. It was founded by

The temple was originally a villa for a member of the Fujiwara, the most powerful family at the court, but later became a monastery. No need to buy postcards to remind yourself what this temple looks like -- just look at the back of a ten-yen coin.

Byodoin is located in the town of **Uji**, just south of Kyoto, but the JTB include it in their full-day Nara itinerary.

Prince Shotoku, the man on the 10,000-yen note.

As the Japanese will tell you proudly, it contains some of the oldest wooden buildings in the world. A hundred years ago nobody gave two hoots. Then, with modernization in full spate, Horyuji's five-story pagoda was almost sold for firewood to the proprietor of a public bath -- for quite a tidy sum, it must be aid. All that prevented the deal going through was that the bath proprietor could not find any way of transporting it.

As valuable as the buildings them-

ABOVE Some of the many lanterns of Nara's Kasuga Shrine.

selves are, the Buddhist statuary they contain is some of the most beautiful in Japan. It's perhaps just as well that no tours, at least no English-speaking ones, call here, for these things deserve lingering over. Many of the best are preserved in the ferro-concrete safety of the temple's **Great Treasure Hall (Daihozoden)**.

Close to Horyuji, almost like an annexe (though it's separate and an admission fee must be paid) is the **Chuguji** convent. This contains the oldest piece of embroidery in Japan, but the main attraction is a statue which brings the Horyuji tour to a fine conclusion, the **Miroku Bosatsu**. This slender, youthful figure, the Buddha of the Future, head tilted forward as if listening, eyelids lowered, fingers of the right hand poised near the cheek, is meditating, we are told, on the sufferings of mankind. It is a soulful work, full of compassion.

On the way to or from Horyuji, if you go by bus, you can visit **Yakushiji**, another famous and ancient temple. Like Horyuji, Yakushiji is noted for its beautiful statues. An English-language booklet available at the entrance tells all.

How To Get To There

As we mentioned above, the quickest and most convenient service to Nara is provided by the Kinki Nippon private line and the fastest service from Kyoto takes about 50 minutes.

Touring Nara

JTB's 8-hour full-day Nara tour visits Byodoin, Todaiji, Kasuga Shrine and Kofukuji Temple as well as Nara Park (the deer park). Departure is from major Kyoto hotels between 8.10 and 9 a.m. and the adult fare is ¥8,800.

The JTB and Fujita both offer afternoon tours calling in at Todaiji, Kasuga Shrine and Nara Park. Pick-up time is between 1.30 and 2 p.m. in Kyoto. Either tour takes four to five hours and the fare is the same for both: ¥4,800 for adults.

All these tours operate daily.

Fujita and Kinki Nippon Tourist also operate combined Kyoto and Nara tours, visiting Kyoto in the morning and Nara in the afternoon. The combined adult fare is ¥7,800 for Fujita and ¥6,200 for Kinki Nippon.

Round trips. It's also possible to begin and end your Kyoto/Nara tour in Tokyo. Both the JTB and Fujita operate one-, two-and three-day round trips, visiting a variety of the attractions that have been detailed for other tours above. Adult fare for the the one-day tour is ¥45,000, for the two-day tour about ¥63,000 and for the three-day tour about ¥75,500. Transport between Tokyo and Kyoto is by Shinkansen.

For more details of these tours and others visit TIC offices in Tokyo or Kyoto.

OSAKA

Kyoto is the city of temples, your guide may tell you, Osaka the city of bridges. True enough, but more strikingly Osaka is the city of factories: there are more than 30,000.

It is the third biggest metropolis in the country after Tokyo and Yokohama and has roughly twice the population of Kyoto. But from the foreign visitor's point of view, it's a long way off challenging either Tokyo or Kyoto as a desirable destination. Tourist attractions are few, the crowds are dense and more aggressive than in the capital, English-language signs are rare, the labyrinthine underground train interchanges are mind-boggling, and the whole texture of the place is coarser and tackier than Tokyo.

In fact it's one of those places, not uncommon in Asia, which bring home to the foreign visitor, with uncomfortable clarity, the fact that they were not

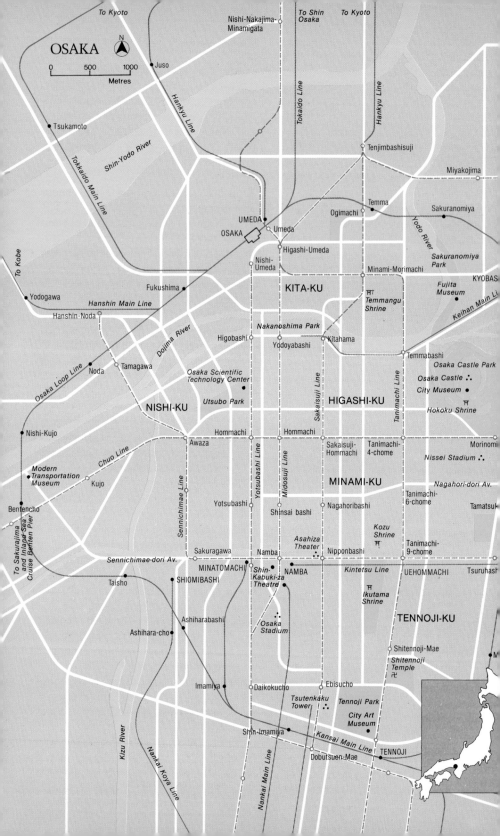

made with him in mind.

The city fathers periodically strive to improve Osaka's image, and their money and determination assure a modicum of success. 1970's World Expo was a recent attempt, and in 1983 a festival to celebrate the 400th anniversary of the foundation of Osaka Castle kicked off a schedule of events designed to keep an international spotlight on the city into the next century. One of the 1983 attractions was a spectacular rally of the tall sailing ships, and each year for the next sixteen there should be fresh surprises. The International Design Festival, which also started up in 1983, takes place every two years.

As well as these special lures, Osaka does have a number of perennial claims to fame. The **Minami** downtown section puts all but Tokyo's most garish quarters in the shade. Good restaurants are innumerable, and the food is remarkable for its good value as well as its flavor. There is a new *kabuki* theater (though it rarely stages *kabuki*) and a world-famous puppet theater, home of *bunraku*. And for innocent extravagance the décor of the underground shopping streets, for example at **Hankyu Sanbangai**, has to be seen to be believed.

In common with other major Japanese cities, Osaka has many hotels, *ryokan* and *minshuku*. For more information on accommodation see **Travelers' Tips**.

Osaka's History

Osaka has been a settlement of importance for some 1,500 years, but it was the great sixteenth-century warlord Hideyoshi who fashioned its modern character.

He not only built his castle, Japan's greatest, on the site where imperial palaces had stood in former times, but he also induced merchants from neighboring areas to move into the city and set up shop there. As a result, during the Edo period it became the most important distribution center in the country, and so it remains today.

Osaka enjoyed fantastic growth in the first half of this century: between 1889 and 1940 the population soared from 500,000 to 3,250,000. Although flattened during the war, it has more than regained its previous prosperity. Though it no longer *teems* in quite the way it used to, its carnal, mercantile character is unchanged.

Seeing the City

Despite its size, Osaka has no foreigner-oriented information office. So although English-language literature is available from the Tourist Information Office (Kanko Annaisho) in the station, it's wise to obtain this from the TIC in Tokyo or Kyoto before setting off.

Daily bus tours, conducted in Japanese, will take you round the city's sights. The booking office is underground in Osaka Umeda station and is hard to find unaided. The sights are not much except for the castle, but the ride around the city on the raised expressway at least gives you the sensation that you are coming to terms with the place. The fare is ¥2,010 and the tour leaves at 9.30 a.m. and 2.05 p.m.

Osaka Castle

Articles have appeared recently in the Japanese press suggesting that **Osaka Castle (Osaka-jo)** is much smaller now than it was before: apparently the man responsible copied the design from an old picture and got the scale wrong.

The castle has been destroyed twice since Hideyoshi built it, first in 1615, the second time in the civil fighting of 1868, and it was rebuilt in 1931 using ferro-concrete. The experience of visiting it is similar to that of visiting Nagoya Castle. Most impressive are the gigantic stones with which the outer walls are constructed.

Unless you are really devout, don't waste your time on Osaka's temples and shrines, not even **Shitennoji Temple**. Theoretically it is the oldest in Japan, having been built in AD 593, 14 years before Horyuji (see above under **Nara**). But the latest rebuilding was rather recent and the temple has all the charm and atmosphere of a matchstick model. Save your legs for the real ones. Kyoto is only 32 minutes down the track.

Ethnological Museum

On the site of 1970's Osaka Expo is the new and splendid **National Museum of Ethnology**. Designed by Kisho Kurokawa, one of Japan's top modern architects, it offers a vivid and enjoyable experience of different cultures around the world. A large library of short video films can be viewed in special capsules by individual visitors. An expansive garden, left over from the expo, is nearby.

The museum is accessible by bus from Senri-Chuo (Midosuji Line) or Minami-Senri (Sukaisuji Line) subway stations and also from Ibaraki station, one stop from Shin-Osaka on the Tokaido line between Osaka and Kyoto.

Takarazuka Revue

A curious theatrical experience awaits you at Takarazuka, one terminus of the private Hankyu railway, 25 km. (16 miles) 34 minutes by express from Umeda station -- the daily matinée performances of the Takarazuka all-female vaudeville troupe.

If you like kick lines, this is the place: Takarazuka must have the best (and longest) in the world! Typical shows consist of old-time Japanese love melodramas (pop *kabuki*), American musicals and fast, furious and highly professional revue material. The cavernous theater holds 4,000, and most of the company's fans are teenage girls.

Takarazuka's shows have the whiff of a rather early stage in Japan's modernization, for while the company's form harks back to an earlier age -- single-sex troupes (mostly male) were the norm until 80 years ago -- its image is determinedly Western. The madly popular stars seem to have been picked partly for their Caucasian facial features.

Takarazuka Family Land, in which the theater is located, has an imaginatively designed zoo, a monorail and an

'Age of the Dinosaurs' feature, among other lures. It's one of the best places in the Osaka area to give the kids a treat.

Osaka At Night

Downtown Osaka is divided simply into two sections, north (**Kita**) and south (**Minami**). While the best ho-

Osaka's baldly functional cityscape OPPOSITE is being leavened by more imaginative buildings like this new department store ABOVE.

tels and the department stores are concentrated in Kita, in the vicinity of Umeda station, Minami is the area to head towards for action at night. Namba station, on Midosuji, Sennichimae and Yotsubashi subway lines, is the best place to start from.

Walk north from Namba and, after a few of the most garishly illuminated blocks in the world, you will reach **Dotonbori**, the pedestrian street which runs east-west parallel with the river of the same name.

Dotonbori has a great concentration of worthy restaurants. The *kuidaore* was a type peculiar to Osaka, a gentleman who ate so extravagantly well that he impoverished himself in the process and Dotonbori was where he did it. Crab, blowfish, *tempura*, *nabe* (stewlike) dishes, *kushi-age* (skewered grilled food), *robatayaki* ... you can tread in his footsteps.

A couple of hundred meters east of where you enter the street, on the left, is a small and somewhat old building with a living tree outside, rare on both

counts. It houses an *oden* establishment which has been on the premises for 200 years (the present building is just post-war) and is a good place to rest your eyes from the glare. The food is good, too, and there is a magnificent illustrated menu with captions in English.

Bunraku

Nearby is Osaka's other premier attraction, the **Asahiza Theater**, home of the **bunraku** puppet troupe. For a description of the work of this unique company see **The Pleasures of Japan**, above. As they often tour it's wise to check with the TIC for details of performances in advance.

If you want to go to the theater directly without doing the Dotonbori promenade, Nipponbashi (Saka-suji subway line) is the nearest station.

Tsutenkaku

The authorities are not particularly keen that foreign visitors know about it, but to the North of Dobutsuen-mae Station, two subway stops south of Namba, is one of the most pungent pleasure quarters in Japan. It centers on the 103-meter (335-ft.)-high tower, **Tsutenkaku**, which is a popular symbol of the city. The surrounding streets are full of people having old-fashioned and often rather low-life fun. Here are the *go* and *shoji* (Japanese chess) and bingo parlors, innumerable small bars, porno cinemas and marvelously cheap restaurants specializing in dangerous delicacies like blowfish. The streets and the nearby Tennoji Zoo are littered with (fairly harmless) drunks and deadbeats but nobody seems to mind,

OPPOSITE LEFT The *taiko bashi* (drum bridge) of Osaka's Sumiyoshi Shrine, threshold of the sacred ground. Osaka's pride: gaudy kimono CENTER, TOP, dazzling neon MIDDLE, the fabulous legs of the Takarazuka kick line BOTTOM.

and on the far side of the zoo, near Tennoji Station, is a concentration of massage parlors and other soft-core cat houses. This area of town is at odds with the image of Osaka as an international city of the 21st century, but it has a great, rather grubby charm of its own.

How To Get There

Hikari trains of the Tokaido Shinkansen take 3 hours 10 minute from Tokyo to Shin-Osaka. Kodama trains take 4 hours 14 minutes (the price is the same). From Shin-Osaka you have to board a local train to make the five-minute journey to Osaka station.

The whole Kyoto-Osaka-Kobe area is crisscrossed with railway lines. The fastest service between Kyoto and Osaka is the Kaisoku train which takes 32 minutes non-stop.

Osaka airport is only 20 minutes by bus from the city centre and is thus an attractive alternative to Tokyo's Narita for some visitors. Buses to Osaka, Kyoto and Kobe are frequent. The service to Kyoto takes about an hour.

Touring Osaka

City bus tours with descriptions in Japanese are mentioned above. One English-language tour starting and finishing in Kyoto guides visitors around the city in the space of an afternoon.

KOBE

Westward along the coast from Osaka is the city of Kobe, a port since the thirteenth century and one of Japan's largest. Like Yokohama and Nagasaki, the constant sea traffic has given Kobe more of a cosmopolitan feeling than other cities, and its dramatic location, stacked up like Hong Kong on mountains rising almost directly from the sea, and its relatively balmy climate, have induced as many as 35,000 foreigners to make the city their home.

It is often said of Kobe that it's a great place to live but not much fun to visit. If you do stay for a few days you will enjoy the fine views of the harbor, the sea and the mountains of Shikoku from Mts. Rokko and Hachibuse. **Mt. Rokko**, the highest peak at 932 metres (3,057 ft.) can be reached by ropeway.

Sannomiya, location (and name) of Kobe's main station, and **Motomachi** are the two principal shopping areas, while **Tor Road**, which goes north from the Daimaru store, has a number of famous restaurants. The many affluent foreign residents make loyal customers, and as a result eating out in Kobe can be a special treat. It's probably the best place to try Kobe beef: the world's most pampered cattle are raised on ranches on the other side of Mt. Rokko.

In 1981 Kobe was the site of the huge expo Portopia, and Kobe Port Island, the man-made island in the harbor on which it was located, still features a fairground and a computer-operated loop train which carries neither driver nor guard. The trains leave from Minami-koen station, which has a direct link with Sannomiya station.

As was mentioned in the Osaka section, above, the Kobe area is richly endowed with public transport. The fastest trains from Kobe to Osaka, leaving from Sannomiya station, take about 30 minutes, while fast trains to Kyoto take about an hour.

Let's leave the hurly-burly of Kansai behind and head for open country -- to be specific, for Toba, home of the cultured pearl and the Ise shrines, the Mecca of Shinto. These attractions are within easy reach of each other in the pastoral Kii Peninsula, just over two hours from Kyoto (or Osaka) by Kinki Nippon Limited Express.

TOBA

Women pearl divers: the phrase, which

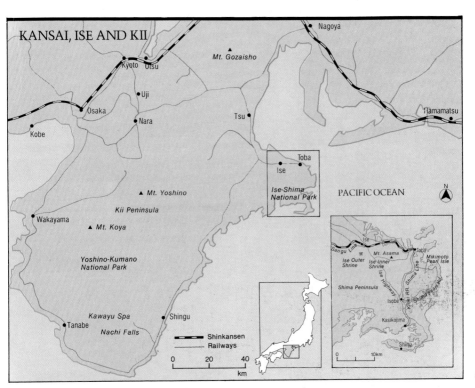

KANSAI, ISE AND KII

Nagoya

Kyoto Otsu
Mt. Gozaisho
Uji
Osaka
Nara
Tsu
Kobe
Hamamatsu

Toba
Ise

Ise-Shima
National Park
PACIFIC OCEAN
N

Mt. Yoshino

Kii Peninsula
Wakayama
Mt. Koya

Yoshino-Kumano
National Park

Sangu Line
Ise Outer Shrine
Mt. Asama
Ise Inner Shrine
Toba
Mikimoto Pearl Isle

Ise Highway
Kinki nR Shima Line
Shima-Pearl Rd

Shima Peninsula
Isobe

Kawayu Spa
Shingu
Tanabe
Nachi Falls
Kasikojima

Shima

Shinkansen
Railways

0   20   40
km

0   10km

summons up only the vaguest of images, stole into one's brain in early childhood, along with the hairy Ainu

ABOVE One of Toba's pearl diving ladies, with bucket and flippers.

and the Abominable Snowman. There's something mysterious and bewitching about them: the lung power, the fish-like grace, some distant link with mermaids perhaps. One longs to know more.

And here's the chance. Toba has been a center of the pearl-gathering trade for a long time, and although pearls are now only rarely dived for, there's enough demand for the many and varied sea vegetables on the sea bottom to keep about 3,500 women divers busy.

You can watch them, by an irony which seems to have passed the Japanese by, at a place called Pearl Island, a sort of shrine to the memory of Kokichi Mikimoto, the father of the cultured pearl -- the man who did more than anyone to put them out of business. They dive there every 40 minutes.

There's an initial disappointment: they don't live up to the disheveled-

geisha image of Utamaro's *ukiyo-e* print; they're well-wrapped up, middle-aged and they smile nicely. But then, leaving their wooden buckets on the surface, they double over like ducks and disappear for whole minutes, then surface again with a plaintive whistling noise. There is something uncanny and fascinating about it.

Elsewhere on the island you can learn how Mikimoto made a fine art, and a fortune, out of torturing oysters, and in **Pearl Hall** you can watch the whole process being enacted, with explanations in English. Some visitors will find they learn more about pearls than they ever wanted to know. But the lady pearl divers make up for it.

'She who cannot support her *tete* husband),' runs one of their sayings, 'cannot claim the name of *yaya* (wife).' A true pearl of wisdom from some redoubtable women.

ISE

A spectacular 40-minute scheduled bus ride over the hills from Toba (Ise-Shima Skyline bus) brings us to the two shrines of Ise, *Ise Jingu* in Japanese, and the very heart of Shinto, the native religion of Japan.

The Victoria Cross (VC) is the highest military honor which can be awarded in Britain, but the medal itself is only made of gunmetal. Similarly these two shrines, Japan's Holy of Holies, are utterly plain, unpainted and undecorated. They are built in the style which prevailed in the country before Chinese techniques of temple-building were transmitted -- with protruding poles, thick thatch roofs and unshaped, though perfect, knotless beams. They represent the most primitive architecture in the land, yet the workmanship is sublimely good, and the atmosphere of sanctity and harmony which blows through the forested precincts like a breeze leaves nobody unmoved.

Strangest of all to Westerners coming from the lands of Stonehenge and Chartres, is the fact that the buildings are less than 20 years old. Every 20 years since they were first built they have been reconstructed on adjacent sites. Despite the huge expense it is intended to maintain this custom indefinitely. The last time it happened was in October 1973. The slow work of gathering timber for the next version has already begun.

Two separate shrines, **Naiku** (the inner) and **Geku** (the outer), about six kilometers (four miles) apart, constitute the Ise shrines. While the outer is dedicated to Toyouke-Omikami, the goddess of farms, harvest food and sericulture, the inner is dedicated to the supreme deity of the Shinto pantheon and mythical forbear of the emperor, the sun goddess, Ameterasu-Omikami.

In both shrines the holiest spot is surrounded by four fences and the public is allowed to penetrate only the first.

Voluptuous roofs OPPOSITE and bald, unpainted *torii* in the grounds of *Naiku*, the inner shrine at Ise.

No photographs are permitted and hats and overcoats should be removed. The area within is reserved for the emperor and shrine officials.

In the inner shrine are preserved the three sacred treasures of the imperial family -- mirror, sword and jewel. The myth goes that the mirror was given by the sun goddess to her grandson when he came down to rule Japan and to father the ancestors of the present emperor.

It is evident that the Ise shrines mean a lot to the Japanese, even the very large number whose belief is faint or

non-existent. The grounds of the shrines are immaculately clean and quiet -- no rubbish, no signs, no Coke machines, no candy-floss merchants. The Japanese can create a spotlessly beautiful environment when they try; one only wishes they tried more often.

A small but much-loved sideshow in this area is the sight of the **wedded rocks** in the sea, about a kilometer (just over half a mile) from Futami-no-Ura station on the JNR line between Ise and Toba. They are linked by a length of sacred straw rope which is replaced in a ceremony that occurs on 5 January every year. They are taken to symbolize Izanagi and Izanami, mythological creators of Japan. They look fine with the sun rising behind them -- patriotic imagery which requires no explanation.

Touring Toba and Ise

A number of regular tours include a visit to Toba and Ise in their itineraries. Fujita Travel's five-day Hakone-Ise-Shima-Kyoto-Nara tour involves a morning here, while the JTB's five-day tour starting from Tokyo and visiting Hakone and Pearl Island on the way to Kyoto and Nara involves a night and the best part of a day in the area. The JTB also offers a full-day tour of the area which starts from both Kyoto and Osaka and winds up in Tokyo. The adult fare for this tour, which departs daily, is ¥36,800. For more information pick up the details in a TIC or JTB office.

Another popular spot which is an easy journey from Kyoto is the old castle town of Himeji, beyond the port city of Kobe to the southwest.

HIMEJI

Shirasagi-jo Castle in Himeji, about 2-1/2 hours by JNR train from Kyoto, is the finest in Japan. The name means 'White Heron', for the castle floats above the town as gracefully as a bird and its color is pure white.

A great many Japanese castles were 'restored' in ferro-concrete during the 50s and 60s, some of them in places where nothing but a plan of the castle remained. This was doubtless good for civic pride (and the construction industry), but it's often a little depressing for visitors, especially when the interior is decked out with lifts and air-conditioning.

There are no such disappointments in store at Himeji. The eight-year repair job completed in 1964 was done with care and tact, and the lavish lifestyle of the original sixteenth-century inhabitants can be readily imagined.

Visit in October and you may be lucky enough to catch the town's **Kenka Matsuri** (Fighting Festival). See the **Festivals** section of **The Cul-**

ture of Japan for details. The castle is a 15-minute walk from Himeji station.

Going further west we leave the Kinki district and enter Chugoku, 'the middle country' as this vitally central region is rightly named.

Here the relatively unchanged northern coast contrasts with the intensive industrial activity of the south, which faces the once-beautiful but now heavily exploited Inland Sea. Yet this southern area, fronting the northern coast of the island of Shikoku, retains a lot of beauty and history too.

KURASHIKI

Kurashiki is a clean and prosperous town near the city of Okayama, 159 km. (99 miles) from Kobe. One section of the town has a strong and peculiar charm which is almost enough to justify a visit: while unmistakably Oriental, it has the atmosphere of an ideal village somewhere in rural Europe, though one can't say quite where. Greece? Spain? Southeast England?

The reason for this is the architecture, the sturdy, handsome whitewashed granaries, with thick plaster walls and charming lattice decorations, which dominate this area. Formerly used for storing rice, they are now lived in and evidently much loved by their owners. They lend the place a coherence and harmony you don't expect to find in Japan.

Then suddenly you are stopped dead -- a Greek temple, in stone! This is the Ohara Art Gallery, and it looks remarkably at home among the rice granaries.

Kurashiki's museums are the other reason why a visit can be highly recommended. There are three of them in this area:

The **Ohara Art Gallery** houses a fabulous collection of Western art, including works by El Greco, Rodin and Picasso. Japanese works of various types and other Oriental pieces are among recent additions.

Kurashiki Folkcraft Museum close by is housed in four granaries and exhibits include folkcraft from Japan and elsewhere.

Kurashiki Archaeological Museum opposite the Folkcraft Museum has more than 1,400 archaeological relics from this area of Japan.

A pleasant stream, fringed with weeping willows, excellent souvenir shops and friendly locals add three extra reasons for putting Kurashiki on your itinerary. The good (not cheap) souvenirs include basketwork, woodwork and pots. There is also a delicious local preserve, persimmons (*kaki*) bound tightly in rope. The locally produced sake is also recommended.

A stone *torii* gate OPPOSITE and quiet, willow-fringed waters ABOVE in Kurashiki.

Only one section of Kurashiki is interesting, so go there directly. It's only ten minutes on foot from the town center. Leave the station by the main exit and follow the raised walkway past the Terminal Hotel building as far as you can go. Descend, go straight ahead at the traffic lights, keep walking to the third set of lights, then turn left. You've arrived.

Touring Kurashiki
A visit to Kurashiki is included in the JTB's three-day Inland Sea package tour.

OKAYAMA

Sixteen kilometers (ten miles) east of Kurashiki is the slightly larger city of **Okayama**, which has one of Japan's three most famous gardens. Called **Korakuen**, it's a brief 1-1/2 km. (one mile) bus ride from the station and is a celebrated example of a garden for strolling. In fact, its grassy expanses give it a slightly occidental feeling, but this is mitigated by the waterfalls, tea cottages and carefully tended pine, maple, plum and cherry trees.

The garden was laid out in 1700. The nearby castle, however, which heightens the picturesque mood of the place, is a reconstruction dating from 1966.

Some 150 km. (93 miles) further west along this coast brings us to Hiroshima.

HIROSHIMA

To people all over the world Hiroshima has come to mean far more than the sum of its parts since it was blown to pieces by an atom bomb in 1945. It is one of the few places in the world to which people flock regardless of the fact that there is almost nothing to see, and that the few 'attractions'

are more like repulsions. Hiroshima and Nagasaki, it could be said, are all that has kept the world straight for the past 40-odd years: two victims exhibited at the entrance to the nuclear road, whose horrible scars have deterred us from venturing further.

In other words there is very little for the visitor in Hiroshima, but it will and should remain a must on any tour of Japan for the indefinite future.

The salient facts are that on 6 August 1945 at 8.15 a.m. a single American bomber dropped an atomic bomb over the city. When it exploded at a height of about 500 meters (1,600 ft.) the temperature in the vicinity rose to 30,000°C (54,000°F). The city was flattened instantly, and of the population of 344,000 (1940 census) about 200,000 lost their lives. Many of those who survived were later to die prematurely of leukaemia and other radiation-induced diseases.

These facts and a great many others, along with paintings, models and debris from the blast, are gathered to-

the Peace Museum: Miyajima Island.

gether in the **Peace Memorial Museum** in Peace Park (**Heiwa Koen**), and this is the place for which visitors should make a beeline (take a bus or tram from the station). The entrance fee is very low, the captions are in English, and the display is vivid.

The museum building and the cenotaph outside are nothing to write home about. Far from evoking the disaster they show the pitiful inadequacy of the vocabulary of modern architecture in the face of it. The statue in Nagasaki's Peace Park is a much braver and more powerful attempt.

Christians will want to see the **Memorial Cathedral for World Peace** near the station, constructed in 1954 due to the efforts of a Belgian priest who survived the blast.

And that's about all. Hiroshima is once again a large and flourishing provincial city, but there is nothing much else to see. However, less than an hour away is a spot which is a balm to the soul after the rigors of

MIYAJIMA

The easiest way to Miyajima is by JNR train from Hiroshima station to Miyajima-guchi. From there to the island it is a short ferry ride. Ferries operated by both JNR and a private company do the run, but the price and journey time are the same.

Miyajima is a wooded and mountainous island with more monkeys and deer than people. Its most famous feature is visible from the ferry when you embark: a large and elaborate red *torii* (shrine gate) set in the sea. You will probably have seen it before in guidebooks or on postcards. This is the gateway to **Itsukushima Shrine**, the island's main attraction. If you pass the ferry trip to the island with your nose in this book you will miss the view popularly believed to be one of the three most beautiful in Japan. It's certainly very pretty.

The island has a strongly numinous atmosphere, like the shrines at Ise Jingu. In the West, churches can, if they are beautiful enough, lend an air of holiness to the places where they are built. Shinto works in reverse: the air of holiness comes first. It is that which often induces the building of the shrine, and such is the case here. Miyajima is a holy island.

After exploring the shrine -- its *noh* stage is the oldest in Japan -- wander in the park which covers the hill immediately behind it. Full of Japanese maples, this area is supremely beautiful in autumn, but at any season when it's not too crowded the meandering walks, the cries of birds and the heavy scent of flowers make it a charming place.

A ropeway takes visitors up to the

OPPOSITE AND ABOVE Hiroshima's atomic bomb dome and arched cenotaph.

141

highest point in the island. The base station is located near the top of the park. Ask for 'ropeway' and you will be pointed in the right direction. It's not cheap -- ¥1,500 -- but it's worth it for the views, Hiroshima on the way up and the silvery waters of the Island Sea from the top. There's a monkey park at the top too, while down near the harbour and the shrine deer wander freely, as at Nara.

Miyajima can be done in half a day, but if you're feeling razzled from too much city why not stay the night and take the time to unwind? There are plenty of places to stay -- hotels, *ryokan* and a youth hostel. You won't find many prettier places in Japan -- or anywhere else.

Touring Hiroshima and Miyajima

JTB organizes a full-day tour to Hiroshima and Miyajima which leaves from Kyoto or Osaka on the morning of every Sunday, Tuesday and Thursday between March and November. These two destinations are also included in the JTB's two-and three-day Inland Sea tours and its seven-day tour of Kyushu and the Inland Sea. Leaflets are available from JTB offices.

NORTH COAST

While the south coast of western Honshu has the most famous sightseeing spots, it also has a great concentration of industry. The north coast is less spectacularly endowed in both respects: placid, rural, with only a few special attractions. Traveling along the coast is simple -- a JNR line runs all the way from Tsuruga, north of Lake Biwa (some two hours north of Kyoto) to Shimonoseki at the southern tip of Honshu. The noteworthy spots along the way are: **Amanohashidate**, about three hours by train from both Kyoto and Tsuruga, one of the three most sce-

nic spots in the country, along with Miyajima (near Hiroshima) and Matsushima (near Sendai). The attraction lies in the pine tree-dotted sandbar which stretches across the entrance of Miyazu Bay and which, when inspected upside down looking through one's legs, is indistinguishable from the sky. It's a *frisson* which may well be overrated. The best view is from **Kasamatsu Park**, accessible from Amanohashidate by bus and ferry. Amanohashidate means 'bridge of heaven'.

Travel along the coast for another three hours and you come to **Tottori**, famous for its 16 km (10 miles) strip of sand dunes, the uncanny atmosphere of which lent such power to the classic Japanese film *Woman in the Dunes* (based on the novel by Kobo Abe, available in translation).

Two and three quarter hours further west is the city of **Matsue**, known for its small but charming seventeenth - century castle. The nineteenth - century American writer and Japanophile Lafcadio Hearn lived here, and his home and effects have been preserved.

Inland from the industrial town of Masuda, some two hours further on, is the station of **Tsuwano**, northern terminus of the Yamaguchi line to **Ogori** (one stop east of Shimonoseki on the Shinkansen), one of the only two lines in the country plied by steam trains ('*esu-eru*' --SL-- for steam locomotive -- Japanese). The service operates from August to December, but not every day; check with the TIC for current details.

Back on the coast, 90 minutes from Masude, is the thriving pottery city of **Hagi**, renowned for the delicate gray glaze of its tea ware which grows richer and deeper with use. The pot-

Views of the shrine on Miyajima, 'shrine island'.
BOTTOM RIGHT the famous *torii* gate in the sea.

143

teries are in the Shoin-jinja area, accessible by bus from Higashi-Hagi station. The remains of a castle and some old streets and houses add to Hagi's interest: it's probably the single most worthwhile spot on this coast.

Shimonoseki, at the end of the line, is the starting-point for the thrice-weekly ferry to Pusan in South Korea. It's also where most of the *fugu* the famous poisonous blowfish, comes from. But to sample that it may be as well to jump across to Kyushu. (There's a *fugu* restaurant listed under Fukuoka, Kyushu's northernmost city, in the **Food** section.)

KYUSHU

Japan's Honshu -- 'Main Island' -- has most of the people, cities and industries which are propelling Japan at full speed into the twenty-first century. It's very exciting, but there are times when you want to escape. The best thing to do then is to jump the island.

You can go north to Hokkaido or south to Kyushu. Either place offers space, peace and country ways, but Hokkaido is Japan's new territory, with a history that goes back only a little over a century.

Kyushu on the other hand, full of splendid natural beauty, also has a long and rich history and offers some of the most rewarding sightseeing in the country. As the nearest point in Japan to the continent, it was in the early days the jumping-off point for immigrants from China and Korea. Recurrently since then it has served as the funnel through which foreign wisdom penetrated the country. At the beginning of the modern period many Kyushu men were in the vanguard of the reform movement.

Kyushu, then, is fully alive to the modern world, but particularly in the south it has so far been spared the intensity of development which marks Honshu. The cities with their colorful trams have a friendly, manageable feeling, and they don't stretch for hundreds of miles. The landscape beyond varies from the domesticated to the stupendous. Much of it is unsullied.

FUKUOKA/HAKATA

Entering Kyushu from the north, through Kitakyushu and Fukuoka, does not fill the visitor with gleeful anticipation, for this part of the island is solidly industrial. The Kitakyushu area, an agglomeration of five cities that were formerly discrete, has been known for centuries for the quality of its steel, and this tradition is upheld in the city's modern steel mills.

Fukuoka is the island's largest city and another center of industrial activity. Strictly speaking, the name Fukuoka describes the section of the city west of the Naka River, while the east side is called Hakata -- which is also the name of the railway station, south-western terminus of the Tokaido Shinkansen.

Fukuoka is also a major port, while the airport, blessedly close to the city center, offers the cheapest and shortest air link to Pusan in South Korea.

The area's Korean connection is also manifest in the pottery-making centers near the city, Koishiwara and Onda, where Korean potters were originally employed.

Fukuoka's few sightseeing attractions need not detain you long: the rest of the island to the south offers many more. But the city has two distinctive and very different features which should be mentioned before we pass on.

OPPOSITE Day and night in Fukuoka/Hakata, Kyushu's raunchy port city.

144

Fifteen minutes on foot north of Hakata station is **Shofukuji**, a temple of the Rinzai Zen sect, which is supposed to have been founded in 1195. If it was, it is the oldest Zen temple in the country. The priest who established it, Eisai, was also responsible for introducing tea into Japan from China.

On a delta about the same distance west of the station is the **Higashi-Nakasu** section of town, the main amusement quarter. As well as conventional entertainments and restaurants, the area has what are believed to be some of the most *risqué* clubs in the land.

Fukuoka is a major transportation centre, offering ready access to all places of interest on the island.

BEPPU

Beppu is one of the biggest hot spring resorts in Japan. Every day as much as 100,000 kiloliters (220 million gallons) of hot water bubbles up out of 3,795 different orifices, and a large town has sprung up to take advantage of this amazing bounty.

Like women pearl divers, mixed bathing has long been one of Japan's semi-legendary attractions for the foreign male, and Beppu has it, or so the rumour goes. It's to be found at **Hoyurando**, a hotel-style resort a kilometre or so to the west of the 'hells' -- naturally occurring pools of boiling water of various lurid colours -- which are the town's most famous draw.

There are two outdoor pools at Hoyurando, the best in Beppu, or so it's said, and both are mixed. It is not necessary to stay at the hotel to use the bath.

One hotel worth splashing out on is the enormous **Suginoi Hotel** (tel: (0977) 24-1141), renowned for its vast baths, housed in glazed structures the size of aircraft hangars (one for each

sex) and with the atmosphere of a tropical hot house in a botanical garden. There are dozens of baths of different sizes, shapes and temperatures, and ornaments include a waterfall, a slide, a *Torii* (gate) and a revolving image of a benignly smiling Buddha.

Also available at Beppu is the famous hot sand bath, *sunayu*. This is to be found at **Takegawa**, near Beppu station. One of the ladies at the bath digs a hole in the naturally hot sand for you. Having undressed, and not forget-

ting your little towel, climb in and the lady will heap more sand around you, up to the neck if you like. The unearthly feeling of relaxation as the heat penetrates to your bones has to be experienced to be believed. And it's not expensive -- only a few hundred yen.

(For more about baths and bath etiquette see the **Baths** section of **The Culture of Japan**.)

The countryside between Beppu on the east and Kumamoto on the west is among the most dramatic on the island. While it can be enjoyed from the train, the trip along Yamanami Highway, which links Beppu with Kumamoto and continues to Nagasaki, is famous for its marvelous views. Whichever way you go, the high point of the trip is Mt. Aso, Japan's most dynamically active volcano.

MT. ASO

The first thing the visitor notices on arriving in the small town of Aso is how extraordinarily flat the tops of the surrounding mountains are; and they are all of uniform height. The reason is

eaten like raw fish, is the local delicacy). A small volcano, grass-green and with an indentation in the crater which might have been made by a huge thumb, comes into view. Round a corner and beyond a lake is the spanking new **Volcano Museum**, opened in July 1982. Video cameras are trained on the active crater: when an eruption takes place it is possible to watch it on screens at the museum.

The bus terminates at Aso-zan Nishi (also West station) from where it's a five-minute ropeway ride or a 15-

that you are standing in the largest volcanic crater of its kind in the world, 24 km. (15 miles) long, 19 km. (11 miles) wide and 120 km. (75 miles) in circumference. Those mountains are the crater's rim. The size of the actual volcano of which in very ancient days this was the active crater boggles the mind. Mt. Fuji would have been a mere mole-hill next to it.

Within this huge crater, as you can see if you take the bus from near the station up to the still-active peak, the countryside is lush and green. Beef cattle and horses graze on the rich grass (raw horsemeat, sliced thin and

minute walk to the edge of the crater. As you climb, the landscape grows grim, gray and lifeless. Concrete shelters with massive walls and roofs begin to appear near the road. On the rubble of the most recent eruptions wisps of grass hang tenuously.

Even so, the vast size and the desolation of the crater come as a shock; despite our knowledge of nuclear weapons, it is hard to comprehend power on

OPPOSITE AND ABOVE Salubrious steam billows out of the ground at Beppu Spa hotels ABOVE are strategically located.

this scale. It's very impressive.

At the bottom of the crater is the bright green lake, steaming continuously. This, the largest of the mountain's five craters, is 600 meters (1,964 ft.) across and 160 meters (524 ft.) deep. Black smoke pours out of it and occasionally deep rumblings can be heard.

The volcano is as deadly as it looks. Dozens have died under the lava during the past few decades. The most recent eruption was in 1979 when three died and 16 were injured. Up to that time it had been possible to approach the volcano from the west, skirt around the crater (by bus) and descend on the east side (or vice-versa), and other guide books describe this possibility. However, since the last disaster the eastern approach has been closed and there is now only one way up and down.

The chances of being done in by the volcano are of course very slight. And the views make it a worthwhile risk.

There are several places to stay in the area, both in Aso itself and in the nearby spas. For details obtain the TIC's mini-guide to the area before setting out.

One hour by train from Aso is **Kumamoto**, the major city in the area. The castle is new, built around 1960, but the city boasts a lovely garden, 20 minutes by bus from Kotsu Center in the middle of town: **Suizenji Park**. It was laid out in 1632 and contains skillful reproductions of famous sights such as Mt. Fuji and Lake Biwa.

The area around Aso is designated as a national park. Another such is the **Unzen-Amakusa National Park** west of the city. This is an area of mountains, islands and tranquil water, and there are several picturesque ways of negotiating it by ferry and bus.

There is one compelling reason for passing this way: it's the road to

ABOVE Oura Catholic Church, near Glover Park, built in 1864. It is the oldest Gothic-style structure in Japan.

148

Nagasaki. A provincial city with a richer history and with more to see than many capitals, Nagasaki is a must. It is simply one of the most fascinating places in Japan.

NAGASAKI

Nagasaki was the world's second A-bomb victim, but unlike Hiroshima it was not completely flattened. In fact, far more than any other Japanese city, Nagasaki is a melting-pot of peoples and cultures, a vivid, city-wide museum of the nation's interaction, during the last 400 years, with the outside world. The city's steep green hills bristle with spires, towers, statues and landmarks.

The city was first created as a port of entry for Western trade in the sixteenth century. It rapidly became a center of both trade and Christianity. That extrovert phase in Japan's history turned out to be a brief interlude, and among the events which brought it to an end the crucifixion of 20 Japanese and six Portuguese Christians in the city was one of the most painful. A relief showing the 26 sainted martyrs stands outside a museum three minutes' walk up the hill opposite the station. The museum has some fascinating early European maps of Japan.

Even when the rest of Japan had severed all contact with the Western world, Nagasaki held on by a single thread. That thread was a small manmade island in the harbour called **Dejima** and here, throughout the nation's 250 years of isolation, a colony of Dutch merchants was maintained and confined.

Dejima is no longer an island -- it's just a couple of stops on the tram from Nagasaki station -- but reconstructions of the old buildings remain as a reminder of the stubbornness of the shogun, and the even more stubborn imperatives of trade.

Nagasaki is an exception to the rule in a country where religions habitually lie down in harmony together: not far from the martyrs' monument is a Buddhist image which clashes violently with it -- on purpose, one suspects. It is a high aluminium figure of Kannon, Buddhist goddess of mercy, and it stands on a tortoise's back. It also helps to remind us that tortoise-shell is one of the city's craft products. A shop which sells delicately crafted tortoise-shell hair clasps and sailing boats is to be found near **Megane (Spectacles) Bridge** -- Japan's first two-arched bridge.

Other figures of Kannon -- tiny, these, and made of porcelain -- can be found in the **Jurokuban-kan Museum** by **Glover Park**. They hold infants in their arms and their startling similarity to figures of the Virgin and Child is not accidental. These images were used by the 'hidden Christians' who, in small islands south of Nagasaki, persisted in their faith throughout the 250 years of the Tokugawa period during which Christianity was proscribed.

As we have noted, Nagasaki was built for trade with the West, and the buildings which are the focus of interest in Glover Park commemorate the second great wave of foreign trading which ushered in Japan's modern age. One of the pioneers was an English entrepreneur called Thomas Blake Glover who settled in the city. He built a pretty little house with a splendid view of Nagasaki Harbor and lived there with his Japanese wife and two children.

It was the first Western-style home in Japan and has been preserved as his shrine. Japanese visitors are impressed by the gigantic size of the rooms, while Westerners find it diminutive and charming -- rather Oriental, in fact, with its delicate posts and fan-shaped rooms on the harbor side. Perhaps Glover thought he had designed a Japanese house.

Glover Park is the one place to go if there is only time to visit one place in Nagasaki -- not so much because of Glover but because of the two museums. They are a treasure-trove of objects, pictures, pots and everyday things of all sorts from all phases of the city's history.

Nagasaki was the most convenient port of entry to Japan for Chinese as well as Westerners, and Chinese culture has penetrated deep into the city's customs and fabric. The bright greens, reds and golds of Chinese Ming and Ching architecture can be seen here and there. A new school of Chinese Zen Buddhism arrived in the city in the seventeenth century and its temples look interestingly garish and extravagant in Japan. There's a small Chinatown in the Tsukimachi district, and some of the city's festivals have a strong Chinese flavor: dragon dances, rowing races and a parade with highly decorated miniature Chinese boats on wheels, packed with musicians, which are pushed through the streets and whirled around at tremendous speed by gangs of muscular boys.

If you miss the festival itself, between 7 and 9 October, console yourself with a visit to the museum in Glover Park where the boats are stored out of season. If you are lucky you may catch a film of the festival at the same place.

Nagasaki's most recent claim to fame was the disaster which occurred on 9 August 1945, three days after Hiroshima, when the second atom bomb to be used exploded 500 metres (1,600 ft.) above Matsuyama in the north of the city, 'instantly mimicking the appearance of another sun in the air'. Nagasaki was only chosen as a target when cloud and smoke prevented the bombing of Kokura in Kitakyushu. The city was a hapless victim, and nearly 80,000 of her citizens died. The huge statue erected in the park at the explosion's epicenter is a powerful injunction not to forget and deserves to be seen.

Touring Nagasaki

Maps and advice about touring the city can be had from the Trade and Tourist Center on the second floor of a large building opposite the south exit of the station. The large sign is in English. The people there are friendly and speak enough English to be helpful. Ask there about city tours -- conducted in Japanese, though an English-language pamphlet is provided -- and also about the ¥500 all-day ticket for the city's tram service.

For details of JTB tours which call at Nagasaki see the end of the Kyushu section.

MIYAZAKI

The further south you go in Kyushu the brighter and balmier it becomes. The landscape starts to glitter. Palm trees line the streets. Some of the tourist traps around here are shameless imitations of popular spots in Hawaii -- and the weather's so good they almost pull it off.

Following the east coast of Kyushu south from Beppu you reach the city of Miyazaki. This was one of the semi-legendary centers of Japan's earliest culture and in **Heiwadai Park**, about 2 km. (1-1/4 miles) from the city center, are to be found many *haniwa*, clay figures which have been excavated from nearby burial mounds.

Miyazaki has great beaches too. The **Nichinan Kaigan** area stretches for about 100 km. (62 miles) south of the city and is one of the best in Japan.

KAGOSHIMA

Satsuma oranges come from here --

Satsuma was the old name of this region. Many of the samurai who ousted the shogun at the start of Japan's modern period came from this city, the most famous being Saigo Takamori, a giant of a man who committed *seppuku* (hara-kiri) with his comrades in a cave in one of the city's parks when his rebellion against the government failed.

The chief attraction at Kagoshima is the active volcano a brief ferry ride from the city on the island of **Sakurajima**, luring visitors while it threatens the populace. On account of the volcanic dust which frequently spews forth from the crater, Kagoshima people are renowned for carrying umbrellas in all weather. You can't get as close to the active peak, **Minami-dake**, as the bravest might wish: too dangerous, they say.

IBUSUKI

An hour or so down the coast from Kagoshima -- trains, buses and hovercraft make the trip -- is the popular hot spring resort of Ibusuki. The town is famous for its hot sand baths -- see **Beppu**, above, for details -- and like other similar places is a center for the sybaritic pleasures of the Japanese, with geishas, cabaret shows and plenty of booze to augment the hot bathing.

BELOW Hot sand bathing at Ibusuki.

151

There is a 'Jungle bath' at Ibusuki's enormous **Kanko Hotel**, which is mixed -- in theory. There is a ladies' entrance but it doesn't seem to be used much. A number of foreign visitors have soaked themselves into a stupor waiting for it to open.

There is pretty country in the vicinity of the town, as there is all over southern Kyushu. Volcanic **Mt. Kaimon** lodges in the memory: perfectly shaped, it sits on the coast like a cone of green incense.

How To Get There

The city of Fukuoka in the north of the islands is the main gateway to Kyushu for travelers from Tokyo. To Fukuoka Airport takes 1 hour from Osaka and 1 hour 40 minutes from Tokyo. The Tokaido Shinkansen ('bullet' train) from Tokyo via Kyoto and Osaka terminates at Hakata, Fukuoka's station, and the journey from Tokyo takes 6 hours 56 minutes. If you start from Kyoto it's possible to take a very nice boat trip through the Inland Sea from Osaka or Kobe, terminating at Beppu.

TOURING KYUSHU

The JTB offers three regular tours to Kyushu. All three depart every Tuesday, Thursday and Saturday between March and November.

The five-day tour leaves from Fukuoka and visits Beppu, Aso, Kumamoto, the Amakusa Islands and Unzen, and Nagasaki, winding up again at Fukuoka.

If you want, you can start this tour from Kyoto or Osaka. It adds some ¥43,000 to the fare but nothing to the length of the tour because, apart from checking in at the hotel in Fukuoka, the first day is free time anyway.

The seven-day tour leaves from Kyoto or Osaka. The first four days follow the same route as the above-mentioned five-day tour. The following three days take in Hiroshima, Miyajima and two other islands in the Inland Sea,

finishing up in Kyoto or Osaka.

Leaflets are available at JTB offices.

DO-IT-YOURSELF

As detailed above, package tours with English-speaking escorts are available to all the places described in this chapter, with the exception of Himeji. But it's quite possible to visit some or all of them under your own steam. The railway network penetrates everywhere and is extremely efficient (though far from cheap). It is augmented by a range of services -- short-and-long-distance buses, trams, cablecars, ropeways, ferries, rickshaws, rentable bicycles -- which make Japan a feast of transportation. There are always places to stay, from impersonal but convenient business hotels to elegant *ryokan* to temple youth hostels. Even in the countryside many people speak enough English to be helpful -- if pushed. Armed with the advice in **Travelers' Tips** you can hardly go wrong.

Here are some suggested itineraries for visitors who want to get as much out of a brief stay as they can:

Two days

Day one: Nikko.
a.m. -- Sightseeing Toshogu Shrine
p.m. -- Bus/taxi to Chuzenji Temple and Kegon waterfall.
Day two: Tokyo.
a.m. -- Visit Imperial Palace East Garden and Hibiya Park; window-shopping in nearby Ginza;
p.m. -- Ginza line subway to eastern terminus, Asakusa, sightseeing at temple and market, then to Ueno (three stops back on Ginza line) for park, temple, museums, zoo. Next stop: Akihabara, two stops from Ueno on Yamanote line, for cheap electrical goods.

Four days

Day one: Nikko (as first day of two-day itinerary).

Day two: Shinkansen from Tokyo to Kyoto.

a.m. -- Call in at the Kyoto TIC for maps and help in booking a room;

p.m. -- See Kyoto's temples and shrines; then traditional Japanese art show at Gion Corner, at 8 p.m. or 9 p.m.

Day three: Nara and Kyoto.

a.m. -- Sightseeing in Nara;

p.m. -- Return to Kyoto, then take sleeping train (*shindaisha*) to Tokyo, leaving Kyoto 12.16 a.m. and arriving Tokyo 7 a.m.

Day four: Tokyo.

Sightseeing as for second day of two-day schedule. Or skip Ueno and fit in an early evening trip to the *Kabuki-za* (pre-book).

Six days

Day one: Tokyo (as second day of two-day itinerary).

Day two: Nikko.

Day three: Kyoto.

Day four: Nara and Kyoto.

Day five:

a.m. -- Shinkansen from Kyoto to Hiroshima; visit Peace Park and Museum;

p.m. -- Miyajima Island, then return to Kyoto.

Day six:

a.m. -- Back to Tokyo;

p.m. -- Meiji Shrine/Harajuku or Akihabara.

Eight Days

As six-day tour, but

Day seven: Kamakura, Gora.

a.m. -- To Kamakura, taxi to Daibutsu (Great Buddha), Zeniarai Benten and back to station;

p.m. -- Kamakura to Ofuna (Yokosuka line), change to Tokaido line Tokkyu (special express) travel to Odawara, gateway to Hakone; Odawara to Gora by Tozan line, stay at Gora Hotel or Suikokan (*ryokan*) tel: (0460) 2-3351 -- book before leaving Tokyo.

Day eight: Hakone.

a.m and p.m. -- explore Hakone area, winding up at Hakone-Yumoto. Take Romance Car of Odakyu line to Shinjuku in central Tokyo. (Last Romance Car leaves at 8.13 p.m., arrives at 9.43 p.m.)

Ten Days

Day one: Tokyo.

Day two: Nikko.

Day three: Kyoto.

Day four: Nara and Kyoto.

Day five: Hiroshima and Miyajima.

Take overnight ferry from Hiroshima to Beppu, leaving 9.p.m. and arriving at 5.30 a.m. (Tickets from Travel Center in Hiroshima Station.)

Day six: all day in Beppu, night in hotel, *ryokan* or youth hostel in the town (book from Kyoto or Tokyo).

Day seven: Mt. Aso, Nagasaki.

a.m. -- Train from Beppu to Aso, visit volcano;

p.m. -- Train via Kumamoto to Nagasaki; stay overnight in Nagasaki (pre-book).

Day eight: Nagasaki, sightseeing; stay another night in the city.

Day nine: Travel to Kurashiki. Train from Nagasaki to Hakata, Shinkansen from Hakata to Okayama, regular train form Okayama to Kurashiki. Sightseeing in Kurashiki. Stay overnight (pre-book) or take sleeping train from Kurashiki to Tokyo, departing Kurashiki at 9.43 p.m., arriving 7.25 a.m.

Day ten: Tokyo.

a.m. -- Train to Okayama, Shinkansen from Okayama to Tokyo;

p.m. -- *Kabuki* at *Kabuki-za* (pre-book) or sightseeing in Meiji Shrine/Harajuku or Akihabara.

Japan: Off the Beaten Track

If you feel like getting out of the tourist rut you are following a great tradition. A hundred years ago Western diplomats delighted in being lugged around the backside of Japan in palanquins. The first person to climb Japan's highest mountain range was an Englishman -- the Japanese had never tried it, believing mountains to be infested with goblins -- and they've been known as the Japan Alps ever since. The chief pleasure in the life of Chicago University Professor Frederick Starr was storming up Mt. Fuji dressed like a native pilgrim in a white tunic, gaiters and straw sandals and carrying a sunshade, crying *'Rokkon Shojo!'* ('May our senses be purified!') and *'Oyama wa seiten!'* ('May the weather in the mountains be good!').

More recently British writer Alan Booth took a summer off to walk the entire length of the country from Hokkaido to Kyushu, raising bewildered eyebrows all the way.

The truth that all these pioneers acted on is that there is as much or more of the real Japan to be found outside the tourist traps as in. There are holy mountains, home of crows, kites and mountain ascetics; pretty towns and villages and farms and festivals, carrying on in much the same way as they always have.

Then there are whole regions like Hokkaido which lack historical interest but display facets of the Japanese landscape and character that are almost unknown outside the country.

A hundred years ago there was the fascination of the totally unknown, the absolutely alien -- but there was the inconvenience of the unknown to contend with as well. Nowadays, even in the remotest hamlet, there are reminders of Japan's white-hot technology -- the microchip factory nestling in the mountains, the robot helping out in the village workshop -- but in compensation there is the ease of getting there.

Japan's transportation system is among the best in the world, and though the places described below are off the foreign tourist track, the roads leading to them have been well-trampled by the Japanese.

Learning to use this system efficiently takes patience and a little basic information. Read **Travelers' Tips** carefully before setting out.

DAY TRIPS FROM TOKYO

You've been in Tokyo a few weeks and you're craving greenery. You've seen Nikko, you've hiked round Hakone, you've paced out every last meter of Yoyogi and Ueno Parks. Where next?

CHICHIBU-TAMA NATIONAL PARK

This park contains bona-fide mountains, it's not hard to get to and, if you set off early, it makes a good one-day outing. Several million other people know this too, so the area is not totally deserted. Beware of sunny Sundays and national holidays.

How To Get There

Take the Chuo line tokubetsu kaisoku (special express) from Tokyo or Shinjuku to Tachikawa. Change at Tachikawa to the Ome line. Board the Ome line train. Tachikawa is the terminus of only a few Chuo trains.

The Ome line which runs alongside the pretty valley of the River Tama offers two attractive possibilities:

Exploring Mt. Mitake. Get off at Mitake station and either walk or take a bus or taxi to the base of Mt. Mitake. (it takes the best part of an hour to walk it). From the base you can either walk to the top or take the cable car. There's an old shrine at the top and very pleasant gentle hiking, as well as several *minshuku*, including one which is thatched. Idyllic weekends have been idled away on this mountain top.

Nippara Shonyu-do. No, this is not a countrified nude show but a terrific complex of icy caves full of stalactites. Take the Ome line to Okutama, the terminus, then the bus to Sho-nyudo. Good hiking around here, too, and places to stay.

Ask the Tokyo TIC for their mini-guide to Okutama for more detailed information on this area.

Mt. Takao. Though not strictly in this park, 600-meter-high Mt. Takao is also very accessible. Its attractions are comparable to Mt. Mitake's, with a cable car running to the summit and varied hiking possibilities once you've got there. Convenient stations for the mountain are Takao on JNR's Chuo Line, and Takaosan-guchi on the private Keio Line which runs from Shinjuku. The latter is right at the foot of the mountain. Yakuo-in, the temple at the mountain's summit, is said to have been founded in the 8th century.

IZU PENINSULA

Want to swim in the sea? It's lovely and warm but can be mucky (June to September) -- in Tokyo Bay the water looks like *miso* (or oxtail) soup. Some of the closest clean beaches are in the Izu Peninsula, part of the **Fuji-Hakone-Izu National Park.**

How To Get There

Take the Shinkansen Kodama (not Hikari) from Tokyo to Atami (55 minutes). JNR and private trains run from Atami via Ito to Shimoda, the peninsula's principal town.

There are noted beaches near Ito in the north of the peninsula, including Usami and Ito itself, and also in the south, near Shimoda: names to remember are **Shirahama** and **Sotoura.**

The railway terminates at Shimoda, but buses will take you round to the pleasantly rustic west coast. If you are lucky your bus conductress may be wearing a kimono and straw sandals. **Matsuzaki** and **Toi** beaches are known for their bathing.

Atami, at the very top of the peninsula, is one of the nation's most popular hot spring resorts and also boasts an art gallery, the **MOA Museum of Art**, five minutes on foot from the station. It is run by a religious organization called

the Church of World Messianity and apparently has a fine collection of Japanese works of art, including woodblock prints and ceramics, many of which are National Treasures and Important Cultural Properties. How and why they found their way into the hands of the Church of World Messianity is for the reader to discover.

The TIC have prepared a mini-guide to the Izu Peninsula.

YOKOHAMA

Thirty minutes from Tokyo by train, Yokohama is the port where a community of Western merchants grew up in the last century. A few of their houses have been preserved in a place called **The Bluff**. Not far away is Yokohama's **Chinatown**, Japan's largest,

ABOVE Yokohama Port and city skyline.

157

with many excellent Chinese restaurants.

Yokohama's **Sankei-en Park** is a landscape garden on a large scale, and has an excellent collection of old buildings, including tea-ceremony cottages, an aristocrat's villa, a three-storey pagoda and a gigantic eighteenth-century farmhouse. Industrial Yokohama is all around but quite out of sight, until you reach the far end of the park and see huge pink gas tanks.

How To Get There
The Tokaido Line from Tokyo station takes just 30 minutes to Yokohama. Transport within Yokohama is a bit fussy. A No. 8 bus from the east side of Yokohama station will take you to Marine Tower, a short walk either to the Bluff or to Chinatown, and on to Sankei-en. For the latter get off at Sankei-en-mae bus stop. In the bus, position yourself close to one of the loudspeakers so you can hear when the stop is announced, then press one of the buzzers.

KAWASAKI
Another collection of interesting old buildings is located on the outskirts of Kawasaki, an industrial city sandwiched between Tokyo and Yokohama. It's called **Niho Minka-en** or Japan Farmhouse Park. In the quiet, wooded grounds are some 20 old thatched farmhouses which have been brought here from various parts of the country. The interiors of many of them may be explored, and upstairs in one is a museum of old farming tools and other equipment.

How To Get There
Take the Odakyu line from Shinjuku to Muko-ga-oka Yuen station, about 30 minutes by express (*kyudo*). Ask a friendly face, '*Nihon Minka-en, doko des' ka?*' ('Where is the Nihon Minka-

en?') when you arrive and you will be pointed in the right direction.

LONGER TRIPS FROM TOKYO

The following trips can be as long or as short as you like, within reason, but you will need to spend at least one night and usually more on the road. If you are anxious about this, enlist the help of Japanese friends (or the TIC if they're not too busy) to book hotels, *ryokan* or *minshuku* before you leave Tokyo.

This is a necessity if you are traveling in mid-August (the *O-bon* holiday season) or over other national holiday periods such as Golden Week (end of April/beginning of May). At such times of year it is also imperative to book train seats well in advance.

If you are traveling off-peak, however, there is no need to book accommodation in advance. As soon as you arrive at the station in the town where you have decided to spend the night, seek out the *Kanko Annaisho* -- Tourist Information Office -- and have them book a hotel, *ryokan* or *minshuku* for you. They will speak enough English to be able to help you satisfactorily.

CLIMBING MT. FUJI

Mt. Fuji is the highest mountain in Japan and by far the most splendid, but during July and August (the open season) it is not a dauntingly hard climb. An athlete, it is said, could leave home in Tokyo in the morning, reach the peak and be home in time for dinner.

Most people prefer to take it at a more leisurely pace, spending a night at the top and greeting the morning sun with a cry of '*Banzai!*'

Here's how to tackle it. Find your way either to Go-gome (Fifth station) on the north side of the mountain or Shin-go-gome (New Fifth station) on the south side. Shin-go-me is the more convenient, as quite a number of buses run there from Gotemba, Mishima and Fujinomiya stations on the Tokaido line from Tokyo.

From Fifth or New Fifth stations it takes five hours or more to the top. Although all sorts of people do the climb, including the blind and the extremely aged, the mountain demands respect. It's bitterly cold at the top, the wind can be fierce, part of the climb requires hauling oneself along by chains, while part of the descent is a sandy slide.

So warm protective clothes, including gloves, are a necessity. Take water along unless you want to buy it on the mountain; take easy-to-carry food such as nuts and raisins, too -- food and

drink are available but they're not cheap.

At the top there are primitive stone shelters where a space on *tatami* mats may be rented for about ¥3,000 a night. Alternatively, you can take a tent. It gets too cold at the top to stay in the open all night.

OPPOSITE Dusk in Yokohama's Sankei-en Park.
ABOVE Watering the pigeons, pampering the poodle.

To avoid having to sleep at the top many people have taken to setting off long after dark and climbing through the night, arriving at the peak or at one of the higher stations -- the eighth has been recommended -- in time to greet the sun. Sunrise on the peak is at 3.40 a.m.

TO KYOTO -- THE BACK WAY

Route: Tokyo -- Matsumoto -- Takayama -- Toyama -- Kanazawa -- Noto Peninsula -- Kanazawa -- Eiheiji

-- Kyoto.

This leisurely route to Kyoto passes through several of the most charming and well-preserved towns and cities in the country.

Matsumoto, a little over four hours from Shinjuku by express, has one of Japan's finest castles. Painted black, it is known as **Crow Castle** in contrast to White Egret Castle at Himeji. The original castle on this site was built in 1504. The present building is not as old as that but is fully authentic.

Once you get inside it's rather like being below deck in an old man-of-war sailing ship: the impression is of massive beams and very little else. Certainly there are no display cases and no lifts, so it's a longish trudge up the six storeys to the top for little reward.

The historical relics which would, if this were a concrete reconstruction like Nagoya's or Osaka's, be on display in the castle are here stored in the **Japan Folklore Library** in the castle's compound. The ticket to the castle admits you to this, too.

Matsumoto also happens to be the home of the Suzuki method of teaching small children how to play musical instruments, and of a brand new museum designed by Kazuo Shinohara, one of Japan's most original architects, devoted entirely to *ukiyo-e* prints.

From the footbridge above the tracks in Matsumoto station a famous panoramic view of the Japan Alps can be enjoyed.

Two hours by train and bus from Matsumoto is **Kamikochi**, center of the **Chubu-Sangaku National Park** and one of the most attractive parts of the northern Alps. This narrow basin is surrounded by high peaks and is the best base for climbing them.

A detour in a southwesterly direction, half-way to Nagoya, brings us to three of Japan's best-preserved villages where, better perhaps than in cities like Kyoto, it is possible to imagine what life was like in the old days.

The closest to Matsumoto, 50 minutes away by the stopping train, is **Narai**. The other two, **Tsumago** and **Magome**, entail a 1 hour 50 minute express train ride to Nagiso and then a brief bus ride. All three are located along the Nakasendo, the old alternative route between Edo and Kyoto, and the *raison d'être* for all three was to provide accommodation for travelers on the road.

As many of the travelers were of

high caste, including the *daimyo* (feudal lords) and their retinues doing the obligatory commuting between their home province and the shogun's capital, the standard of some of the inns was very high. Interspersed among the inns were craft workshops turning out exquisite souvenirs and everyday articles, and tea houses. In fact, the villages were quite different from the typical farmer's villages in the countryside and more like fragments of the metropolis set down in the wilds.

done. Modern-looking structures are very few, and when a new building goes up -- a post office in Narai, for example -- it's in the traditional style and traditional materials. And very charming it is, too.

A night in a *minshuku* or *ryokan* in one of these villages is perfect time travel. After a hot dip in the tiny bathrooms, in which everything is made of *hinoki* (Japanese cypress), there may be time for a stroll before supper. Array yourself in the *yukata* (cotton ki-

TO KYOTO —
THE BACK WAY

The villagers have rather miraculously managed a smooth transition from feu-dal days to the present. Their economic activity remains almost exactly what it was -- inns, crafts and tea (and now coffee) -- but today the clients are ordinary modern Japanese in search of one of modern Japan's strongest reminders of the past.

Some wise souls have realized that the survival of the villages depends on their maintaining their historical appearance, and this is what they have

mono), *haori* (half-coat) and *geta* (wooden shoes) provided by the *ryokan* (take a parasol if it's raining) and explore the village's single street. Note how narrow the houses are at the front, but how deep: houses were taxed according to the width of their frontage. Note also the small front doors covered with *shoji* paper and

OPPOSITE AND ABOVE Two views of Matsumoto's Crow Castle *Karasu-jo.*

the narrow wooden bars on the upper windows.

You can deepen your understanding of the place the following morning by dropping into one of several *shiryokan*, houses typical of the village whose antique appearance has been preserved inside as well as out. The kettle hangs over the hearth, the abacus is ready by the desk, the second floor is full of silk-weaving equipment.

Craftsmen, including makers of lacquered vessels and combs, are still at work in the villages.

While Narai is out on its own, Tsumago and Magome are connected by the old Nakasendo road. The walk between them takes about three hours and is pleasant, particularly if you go from Tsumago to Magome, as that way the road is largely downhill.

Takayama, accessible without much difficulty both from Matsumoto (some 50 km. -- 31 miles -- away), and from the villages mentioned above, is an elegant and prosperous city, a 'little Kyoto' (like Kanazawa, described below) with a number of strong and unique attractions.

The street of shops and workshops parallel to the river and just east of it (the further side coming from the station) called **Kami-San-no-machi** is beautiful in the severe, classical Edo manner, and an excellent place to find souvenirs: sake (from the brewery), *miso* (from the factory), fine textiles, wooden objects, antiques ... The town is dotted with small sake factories, and if you approach them nicely (and ideally in Japanese) the owners of some of them may be willing to show you around -- a fascinating experience.

The city has plenty of *ryokan* and hotels, and if you stay overnight you can catch the outdoor vegetable and flower market in the morning. Or rather markets, for there are two locations: one by the river and one in front of a historic building called **Takayama Jinja**.

Takayama Jinya, the town's administrative office from about 1700 to 1868, is a must for anybody interested in Japanese history. Shrines, temples and castles -- these are the three types of ancient structures which are readily encountered in Japan. Takayama Jinya is a great rarity, being the only one of 60 administrative offices of the Edo period still standing.

It's a large, rambling building with a garden full of trees swathed in straw bandages (in winter). Admire the roof of cypress bark, the storerooms for rice (the unit of currency and taxation), the large *tatami*-matted reception rooms. Takayama was directly under the domain of the Tokugawa shogun, which was one of the prime reasons for the city's prosperity: this building was the seat of his delegate's authority.

OPPOSITE A restaurant in the post town of Narai.
ABOVE A vermilion bridge in Takayama.

Takayama is an ideal size for exploring by bicycle. There are bike rental shops near the station -- price about ¥250 per hour -- and the Tourist Information people in the station will point you in the right direction. With the help of their map you will also be able to find the **Hida Old House Reservation**, 15 minutes southwest of the station by bike (five minutes by bus or taxi).

It's one of the biggest such parks in the country and may well be the best, with houses of many different types

Second, the place is as phoney as Disneyland because no one lives here. The atmosphere is dead. The old streets in the middle of Takayama, or a village like Narai, give a much stronger sense of living tradition.

There is a shrine in this phoney old village. A question for the proprietors: when you move a shrine bodily to an old house reservation, does the enshrined god oblige by tagging along too?

Entrance to the reservation is ¥300

and several different social strata. It's permitted to poke around inside the houses, so vivid impressions of rural life in the old days can be obtained. The **Wakayama House**, one of the smaller group of houses near the ticket office, has a collection of old spinning, weaving and cooking equipment. The house itself has a steeply pitched thatched roof in the *gasshozukuri* ('praying hands') style.

One has only two reservations about the reservation: first, the friendly jumble of houses of different types can give a confusing impression of old-time social realities. In actual fact all the houses come from very different sections of different towns and villages; no real village ever looked like this.

(children half-price). The English pamphlet is informative.

Magnificent festivals are held in Takayama every April and October. See the **Festivals** section of **The Culture of Japan** for details. Four of the huge and gorgeously decorated festival wagons (*yatai*) are on permanent display in the **Takayama Yatai Kaikan** in the grounds of **Hachiman Shrine**, near the centre of town.

Some 15 km. (9 miles) north of Takayama on the road to Toyama is the small city of **Furukawa** which shares

ABOVE Takayama's morning market and RIGHT a roadside stall in Kyoto.

some of Takayama's antique charms: old atmospheric streets, richly ornamented wagons and a fine festival (19-20 April) during which they are displayed.

The city of **Toyama**, north of Takayama, need not detain you long, but deep in the mountains, 1-1/2 hours by bus west of the city, an amazing institution has been started up: a festival of international theater, based on two new theaters in the village of **Togamura**, one inside an old *gasshozukuri* farmhouse, the other an outdoor stage of the Greek type. The first festival, featuring some of the world's most eminent fringe theater groups, took place in summer 1982. The following year's event was less ambitious and the guests less industrious, and exactly how it will develop is unclear, but the presence of eminent director Tadashi Suzuki alone ensures theater-loves of a worthwhile experience. Take the train from Toyama to Etchu-Yatsuo, then a bus to Toga-Mura.

Like Takayama, **Kanazawa**, 50 km. (31 miles) west of Toyama, is often compared with Kyoto. But this sizable city has a special atmosphere of its own.

For centuries it was the seat of the Maeda clan who ruled the city with a light and civilised hand, encouraging literature, silk-dyeing and other cultured pursuits. Their influence lingers on. Though in 'the back of Japan' there is no sense here of being stuck in the sticks.

Kenroku-en is a large and exquisite landscape garden near the city center. With its ponds and streams, grotesque pines, charming views and tea cottages, it is arguably the most beautiful garden of its type in Japan. Many other people think so, too. If you go expecting peace and quiet you will be scandalized by the crowds and the hubbub. Go expecting Shinjuku station and you may be impressed by how nicely everyone behaves.

In one corner of the garden is **Seison-kaku**, a ravishingly beautiful traditional villa, well worth the admission fee. Wander through its rooms, admire the bold decorative scheme upstairs, sit on the verandah and enjoy the placid garden: the lifestyle of the aristorcrats who used to live here is quite easy to imagine -- and quite enviable.

Bits of Kanazawa Castle survive close by, but more interesting is the small but very well-defined area of old samurai houses called **Nagamachi**. It is easily recognised by the long, high walls of packed earth which enclose the houses. There are old tea shops in this small section and a silk-dyeing workshop. You can watch the craftsmen and craftswomen at work.

There are several other things worth seeing and doing in Kanazawa. The city has recently published an excellent English-language guidebook, titled *Kanazawa -- the Other Side of Japan*, and Tokyo TIC have a mini-guide to the area as well.

Kanazawa is the gateway to the placid and rural **Noto Peninsula**. The train from Kanazawa to Hakui and the bus from there northwards will bring you to **Monzen**, a small town with a beautiful and urbane Zen temple, **Sojiji**. Much of the way there the bus runs along the coast. The fantastic rock formations -- phaluses, doughnuts, pinnacles joined by holy rope -- the old-fashioned prosperity of the little villages with their shiny black roofs, the *wakame* (seaweed) drying by the roadside, the sleek-prowed fishing boats, all help to make the journey a memorable one.

Wajima, the small city north of Monzen, is noted for its pretty lacquer ware. From there express trains will take you back to Kanazawa and on to Fukui. From Fukui take a train -- or a taxi after 3 p.m. or so -- to **Eiheiji**, the main temple of the Soto Zen sect. It was founded by Zen Master Dogen who brought the teachings of Soto Zen to Japan.

> The landscape of the mountains -
> The sound of streams -
> All are the body and voice of Buddha,

is one of Dogen's famous sayings. He's one of Japan's authentic saints.

The temple's location among great cryptomeria trees is awe-inspiring; the only pity is that its fame has turned it into something of a machine for tourists. If you are interested in Zen, try engaging the young monk who hands you the English-language pamphlet in conversation. He may be friendly and eager to talk.

There: you've done it. Returning to Fukui you are poised for the descent to Kyoto, going by way of Tsuruga and Lake Biwa.

The track described above may well be on the way to becoming beaten: in 1982 the JTB offered for the first time a tour which visits several of the places mentioned. The five-day tour starts from Tokyo every Tuesday between April and November and visits Matsumoto, Takayama, Kanazawa and the Noto Peninsula on the way to Kyoto. A leaflet is obtainable from offices of the JTB or TIC.

THE NARROW ROAD TO THE DEEP NORTH

Broken in health and dressed in the robes of a monk, the great lyric poet Matsuo Basho set off from Edo (Tokyo) in 1689, with one disciple, for the perilous regions of the north.

He was on the road for five months. The book -- poems and prose travel sketches -- which resulted was first published in English some eighteen years ago as *The Narrow Road to the Deep North*. Since then that phrase has entered the language; it seems to encapsulate one aspect of the Orient, conjuring up images of high cliffs, deep gorges and tiny figures toiling up winding mountain paths.

Well, where is that narrow road? Where does it lead? What is it like?

It starts, conveniently enough, from Tokyo and goes north some 400 km. (250 miles) as far as present-day Akita Prefecture. Many of the spots that charmed Basho have disappeared under a blanket of industry. Some survive practically unchanged, however. Others have sprung into existence since Basho's day.

Taking his map as our text and leap-frogging and making detours at will, we can put together a fine tour of **Tohoku**, Honshu's northern quarter, an all but undiscovered zone for the foreign tourist. At the same time we can enjoy the thoroughly modern pleasures of the Green-and-white Shinkansen which runs from Ueno in central Tokyo (the platforms are underground) to Morioka in Iwate Prefecture. Details at the end of this section.

Nikko was one of his early stops and is described in **Japan: The Broad Highway.**

Going north from Nikko there is nothing much to detain us before Fukushima. East of this city and accessible by bus is a spectacular area Basho knew nothing of -- for it didn't exist.

In 1888 the volcanic Mt. Bandai exploded with stupendous violence, destroying 11 villages and killing hundreds of people. The discharged rock blocked the courses of local rivers, creating an area of ponds and marshes. This is of peculiar beauty because the water of each of the ponds is a different color. A pretty nature course runs around and between five of them.

This area, called **Goshikinuma**, is very popular with Japanese tourists and should be avoided at weekends and national holidays. It's about 270 km. (168 miles) from Tokyo.

The Bandai-Azuma Skyline toll-road which covers the distance between Goshikinuma and Fukushima features spectacular scenery.

Sendai is the next stop going north, about 350 km. (220 miles) from Tokyo, a historic city whose interest disappeared under wartime bombs. Now it is vigorous and prosperous and looking good, tackling the modern age with confidence.

Forty minutes by train from the city is **Matsushima**, one of the 'three most scenic spots in Japan' (Miyajima near Hiroshima, described in **Japan: The Broad Highway**, is another). Basho visited Matsushima, and so should you. The calm waters of the bay are dotted for miles with islands and islets, and each island is crowned with pine trees. It is indeed beautiful and rather otherworldly. You can take a pleasure boat around the bay to inspect the islands more closely.

Some two hours by train and half an hour by ferry north of Sendai is the small island of **Kinkazan**, at the tip of the Ojika Peninsula. It's a tranquil place of forests, with monkeys and deer running free. There's a large shrine, **Koganeyama-jinja**, which attracts many visitors, and the whole island has a slightly uncanny, numinous atmosphere like that of Miyajima, near Hiroshima. The island's youth hostel is near the shrine. The island makes an excellent retreat for anybody wanting a weekend away from urban frenzy. *Kinkazan* means 'Gold Flower Mountain', probably a reference to the fragments of mica which sparkle in the island's rock.

The best ferry service to Kinkazan is from the port of Ayukawa, reached by bus from Ishinomaki, terminus of JNR's Senseki line from Sendai. One ferry per day also sails from Ishinomaki itself.

From Sendai the Senzan line takes you due west into neighboring Yamagata Prefecture. The stop to watch for is **Yamadera**, which means 'Mountain Temple', and the temple is the attraction. It is perched on a spectacular hill of massive boulders covered with moss from which ancient pines and cypresses sprout at crazy angles. It is one of the most curious sites for a temple in the country, and it is also the place where Basho wrote one of his famous haiku:

So silent!
The cicada's cry
Penetrates the rocks.*

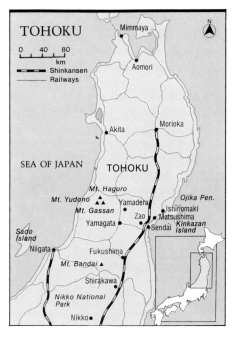

The western part of Yamagata Prefecture is a tranquil area, greatly depopulated and full of natural beauty. The tour ends here, with the three holy mountains which Basho climbed. All three still attract surprisingly large numbers of pilgrims and one of them, **Mt. Haguro**, is a treat for anybody.

Of the first two **Mt. Yudono** is really an extrusion of **Mt. Gassan**. Both are bitterly cold places of fierce wind and driving rain, even in summer.

Mt. Haguro, some 20 km. (12 miles) to the north, is by contrast a placid, gentle peak, though possessing that atmosphere of spirituality that was earlier noted at Ise Jingu and Miyajima (see **The Broad Highway**). A high pagoda, unpainted, stands in forested isolation at the foot of the peak. A stairway of shallow, aged steps makes for a pleasant climb to the top, and half-way there, if you break away from the path and walk for a short distance, is the site of the Southern Valley Temple, where Basho stayed overnight. It's a pleasant spot for a picnic. Nearby a stone tablet bears the words of the haiku he wrote when he was there:

> The summer breeze
> in this blessed southern valley
> bears the fragrance of snow.*

Upon reaching the top of the mountain your eyes are greeted by a multitude of shrines-cum-temples, the chief of which has a roof of incredibly thick thatch. Relax in this, one of the most pleasant spots in northern Japan, and listen to the plaintive music of the holy mountain as an old mountain ascetic, dressed all in white, blows on a huge conch.

The Tohoku Shinkansen

Since summer 1982 the 'bullet' train has been going north, bringing Tohoku remarkably close to Tokyo. Capable of a maximum speed of 210 k.p.h. (130 m.p.h.), the new green-and-white trains are boarded at underground platforms in Ueno in Central Tokyo. The fastest expresses, called 'Yamabiko', equivalent to the 'Hikari' service on the Tokaido Shinkansen, will deliver you to Fukushima in 1 hour 27 minutes, Sendai in just under two hours, and Morioka, the terminus, in less than three. Stopping Yamabiko, which are more numerous, take a little longer. 'Aoba' trains, which terminate at Sendai, stop at all stations along the route,

* Translations of Basho's haiku on this and previous page by the author.

including Shiroishi Zao, gateway to an area famous for skiing.

Yet another Shinkansen service opened in 1982, this one running between Tokyo and Niigata, the city on the Japan Sea opposite Sado Island, mentioned in **Other Islands**, below. This train, the Joetsu Shinkansen, cuts the journey time to Niigata from 3 hours 55 minutes to less than two hours (fastest trains). As the jet foil from Niigata to Sado takes only one hour, this picturesque island to which political dissidents were formerly exiled has suddenly become accessible for summer weekend trips.

The Niigata service came into operation on 15 November 1982, with 21 trains per day. On the same date the number of 'bullets' heading north to Morioka jumped from 14 to 24.

In fact the new Shinkansen services are likely to put a large dent in the reputation this area has long had of being in the back of beyond. Impoverished, remote, in modern times losing much of its population to the cities further south, there is little in Tohoku to make a visit imperative, but its very remoteness will be an attraction for the intrepid. As getting around in these parts requires more detailed information than can be encompassed in a book of this size, it would be a good idea for the visitor to arm himself with a copy of *Exploring Tohoku* by Jan Brown. Tohoku's biggest attractions are undoubtedly the three great summer festivals, held in Sendai, Akita and Aomori (see **Festivals** in **The Culture of Japan**).

HOKKAIDO

Hokkaido is Japan's most northerly large island and has only been developed in earnest since the onset of modernization. It is the home of the very small unabsorbed remnants of three different aboriginal peoples, the Ainu, the Gilyak and the Oroke, but the only remaining tribal activity is laid on for tourists.

Hokkaido's lack of historical interest is made up for by its spaciousness and relative emptiness -- it has 22 per cent of the nation's total land area but only five per cent of the population -- and its pleasant reminders, for Westerners, of home: rolling green meadows spotted with cows and waving fields of grain. The towns seem as American-inspired

poro, the capital, was the site of the Winter Olympics some years ago.

There are three popular areas, all three designated national parks.

In the southwest is **Shikotsu-Toya National Park**. The two lakes, Shikotsu and Toya, are the attraction here, plus the spa town of **Noboribetsu**. Noboribetsu is famous for the mixed bathing which is to be enjoyed at **Dai-Ichi Takimoto Hotel**. It is one of the very few mixed baths in the country which is operational and in full swing.

as the agriculture: they spread on and on.

Due partly to the spaciousness, the people of Hokkaido enjoy a reputation for being looser and franker than other Japanese. Another reason for this is that, drawn as the population is drawn from all parts of the country, the old-fashioned, soil-rooted clannishness prevalent elsewhere has been unable to survive.

The island is great for hiking and camping holidays, particularly in summer when the weather is pleasantly cool compared to the rest of the country. In winter skiers flock here: Sap-

That is, the fair sex use it, too. The bath is enormous and has nearly 20 large pools.

Daisetsuzan National Park, north of the center of the island, offers mile after mile of fairly undemanding and very enjoyable hiking. It's very popular with young Japanese, and hostels are often crowded in summer. Ski here in winter.

The dramatic remains of past volcanic activity dominate the area around Kutcharo in the north of **Akan National**

ABOVE Tokaido Line 'shinks' between Tokyo and Hakata. The new ones going north are painted green and white.

Park. The town of **Akankokan** to the west of the smaller Lake Akan features an Ainu village where tribespeople can be observed doing tribal things. Phony, but perhaps interesting anyway.

SAPPORO

Laid out in a grid pattern like Nagoya and traversed by a subway system, Sapporo is superficially an unlovely city which nonetheless has quite a lot going for it. The night-life, centered in the

Susukino district, is said to be the hottest north of Tokyo, and the city has more than 3,500 bars and cabarets.

Also like Nagoya, the city's central park is a block-wide strip, stretching from east to west. At the east end is the 147 meter (481 ft.)-high TV tower from which there is a'fine view of the city and the mountains beyond.

Winter skiing and the February Ice Festival (see the **Festivals** section of **The Culture of Japan**) are the most common reasons for visiting. The city is said to be a very pleasant place to live.

Sapporo ABOVE is the focal point for skiing and hiking in Hokkaido.

How To Get There

Planes, trains and boats all go to Hokkaido from Tokyo. For most visitors the plane service from Haneda is the most practical.

An interesting alternative for those with time to spare is the ferry service which, leaving from Tokyo Bay at 11.30 in the evening arrives in Tomakomai at 6.45 in the morning, 31 hours 15 minutes later. The service only operates in summer. When the present writer made this trip he did so in the company of several tattooed gangsters and a party of Alaskan Indians. We all enjoyed a game of bingo together in the evening.

SHIKOKU AND THE INLAND SEA

Shikoku is the smallest of the four main islands of the archipelago and is separated from southern Honshu by the picturesque but much-exploited Inland Sea (**Seto Naikai**). It is a placid, unhurried island with a beautiful south coast, which is popular with divers, and some marvelous festivals. There are not as many tourist draws as in Honshu or Kyushu which means that, like the northern coast of southern Honshu, it is an ideal place for the traveler who wishes to become familiar with the texture of everyday rural life. Shikoku is far from being an unspoiled paradise, however, and the light industrial skirts of the towns and cities sprawl as badly as anywhere else.

Takamatsu is the island's principal city, with a population above 250,000. The large, walled park two kilometers south of the station **Ritsurin Koen** is the best thing to see in the city. There are tea cottages, grassy lawns and ponds with ornamental fowl, all wrought into pleasing harmony with pine-dotted rocks in the background.

Near the station and facing the Inland Sea is **Tamamo Park**, where what's left of the city's castle stands --

what's left of the city's castle stands -- which is not much. Admission is ¥20, which makes it very good value. One hour and 20 minutes distant to the southeast by the fastest train is **Tokushima**, a city a little smaller than Takamatsu, rightly renowned for its summer festival (see **Festivals** under **The Culture of Japan**). It is also the starting point of the island's famous pilgrimage course, which takes in 88 of the island's temples. A pilgrimage to each of these in turn is a popular folk-cure for all sorts of problems and a good way of endearing oneself to the gods in general.

People usually embark on such a pilgrimage after retirement. In the old days pilgrims used to hike from temple to temple and the whole course would take some two months. Now most of them go by bus and it takes about a week. They still dress completely in white. Spring and autumn are the most likely seasons in which to spot pilgrims (*o-henro san* in Japanese).

The major city in the south of the island, capital of the prefecture of the same name, is **Kochi**. It's about 2-1/2 hours from Takamatsu by the fastest train. The best thing in the city is the small but perfect castle, built in 1753, perched at the top of a steep slope about two kilometers (1-1/2 miles) from the station. Some of the castle's interesting exhibits include some first, wobbly attempts at Roman calligraphy, pre-modern toys (wooden whales on wheels) and impressive photos, blown up to enormous size, of the castle's nineteenth-century samurai proprietors, looking as fierce and noble as American Indians.

Stretching from the castle gate one kilometer (just over half a mile) east of the castle is a large open-air market, held every Sunday, with a history going back 300 years.

Thirteen kilometers (eight miles) southeast of Kochi, accessible by bus from Kochi station, is **Katsurahama**

beach. With its pine trees, white sand and excellent swimming, it is a typical section of the agreeable coastline of southern Shikoku.

On the route between Takamatsu and Kochi are several temples and shrines worth knowing about. **Zentsuji Temple**, 1.2 km. (3/4 mile) from Zentsuji station, unusually spacious and with a fine five-storey pagoda, is known as the birthplace of Kobo Daishi, one of Japan's greatest teachers of Buddhism. The temple was founded in 813.

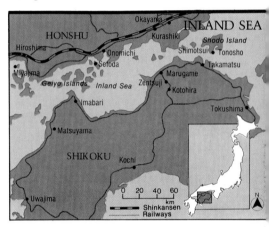

Kotohira, just five kilometers south of Zentsuji, is famous for its shrine of the same name, one of the most revered in the country, which is reached by a one-hour ascent of granite steps.

Uwajima, at the western extreme of the island and accessible by rail from the north or south, is famous for its bloodless bullfighting, in which two of the beasts lock horns and strive to push each other backwards in the sumo style. The sport takes place six times a year: check with the TIC for details.

Shikoku's most populous city is **Matsuyama**, north of Uwajima. Two hours 45 minutes by limited express from Takamatsu and three hours by sea from Hiroshima, it has two main attractions: a castle with a three-storey *donjon* in the center of the city, one of Japan's best-preserved; and **Dogo On-**

sen, an ancient spa housed in an old wooden building 15 minutes from the station by bus or tram.

THE INLAND SEA

The sea which divides Honshu, Shikoku and Kyushu is the birthplace, they say, of the Japanese sense of beauty. And in the scaly seas, the mists, the fishing boats, the shifting perspective of pine tree-prickly islets and islands, there is certainly something quintessentially Japanese, something which invites depiction in *sumie* ink rather than oils.

But, as Donald Richie lamented in his marvelous book *The Inland Sea*, much of the area's beauty is vanishing under a slick of industry. Nothing has happened in the past ten years to reverse that trend, but there is plenty of charm left.

There are two principal ways to enjoy the Inland Sea: by spying on it from a height, and by traveling through it by ship.

High spots with excellent views are Miyajima (see Hiroshima in **Japan: The Broad Highway**), Onomichi and Washuzan Hill.

Onomichi is half-way between Okayama and Hiroshima. A 20-minute bus ride to Nagaeguchi followed by cable car ride brings you to the observatory in **Senkoji Park**, from which there is a great view of the Geiyo Islands.

Washuzan Hill is on the eastern edge of Shimotsui, south of Kurashiki (see **Japan: The Broad Highway**). Buses run directly from Kurashiki, taking about 80 minutes. Shimotsui is itself a pleasant fishing village, from which frequent ferries run to Marugame on Shikoku.

Many ferries ply between various points on the sea's coasts, and details are to be found in the TIC's miniguide to the Inland Sea. Three of the long-distance ferries which pass through many of the pretty spots during daylight hours (in summer -- and you may have to get up early!) are as follows:
Osaka/Kobe -- Beppu
Hiuga (in Kyushu) -- Kobe
Shibushi (in southern Kyushu) -- Osaka

Shorter trips which are recommended include the following:
Shimotsui -- Tomari -- Marugame
Onomichi -- Setoda -- Imabari
Hiroshima -- Imabari
Onomichi -- Matsuyama

For times of all these ferries check the comprehensive train/bus/ferry timetable published monthly and titled *Jikokuhyo* (unfortunately available only in Japanese).

A third way of getting acquainted with the Inland Sea is by spending time on one of its many islands. **Shodoshima** (Shodo Island) is a good place to start: it has a dramatic gorge, lovely countryside, a monkey park and convenient buses to haul visitors between these attractions. It also has olive groves, one of a number of similarities between the Inland Sea and the comparably mist- and myth-steeped Aegean.

Ferries call at three ports on Shodoshima -- Tonosho, Ikeda and Fukuda -- linking the island with major cities in Shikoku and Honshu, including Takamatsu and Kobe.

OTHER ISLANDS

There is almost no end to the islands of Japan. **Sado**, the fifth largest, though much smaller than Shikoku and located off the coast of Niigate in the north of Honshu, is a delightful backwater, renowned for folk dancing, pup-

OPPOSITE Takamatsu's Ritsurin Koen (Park).

172

Classical architecture TOP and surrounding OPPO-
SITE in Ritsurin Koen, Takamatsu. BOTTOM Islands emerging from the mist, a sea of beaten
bronze... the Inland Sea.

pet plays and cuttlefish. It also offers excellent hiking.

Oshima and the other, smaller islands of the Izu chain are close enough to Tokyo to be viable for weekend escapes. There are two live volcanoes and a number of good beaches on them.

Okinawa and the other islands to the south of Kyushu deserve a volume to themselves. The islands have only been integrated into the Japanese state since the nineteenth century, and the native language is incomprehensible to mainland Japanese. The culture is also strikingly different, and the rich colors and strong patterns of Okinawan textiles suggest the ardor and pride of the people. The folk pottery is also famous and was one of the inspirations of Japan's Folkcraft Movement.

The scene of one of World War II's bloodiest battles, Okinawa was only returned to Japan by the USA in 1972, and American troop presence there is still heavy. However, the near-tropical weather and the good beaches have made the island a popular target for Japanese tourists.

Naha, with a population of around 300,000, is the largest city in the island chain and Okinawa's political and economic center. The plane journey from Tokyo to Naha takes 2 hours 30 minutes. Completely destroyed in the war, Naha has been rapidly rebuilt and is not substantially different from other modern Japanese cities.

Eighteen hours away by boat is the island of **Ishigaki**, gateway to one of the area's major attractions, the **Iriomote National Park**, a 290 sq. km. (180 sq. miles) area consisting of the island of Iriomote -- perhaps the wildest spot in Japan. Ninety per cent of Iriomote is covered by primeval jungle, the haunt of wild boar and the last surviving members of a unique variety of wild cat, the *yama neko* (mountain cat).

Travelers' Tips

ARRIVING

You can enter Honshu, Japan's main island, by any one of five international airports: Tokyo (Narita and Haneda), Niigata, Nagoya or Osaka. Osaka is the handiest port for Kyoto, while both Niigata (from 15 November 1982, when the new branch of the Shinkansen opened) and Nagoya are not much more than two hours from the capital. Tokyo's Narita, however, is the port through which most people enter the country. Haneda, Tokyo's old international airport, is now only used by VIPs and Taiwan's China Airlines (so as not to annoy Peking). It is much missed: it was only a 15-minute monorail ride from the center of town; Narita is 66 km. out in the country.

VISAS AND WHATNOT

Japan has visa exemption agreements with 46 countries, including most countries of Western Europe and New Zealand but excluding the United States, Canada, Australia, India and most socialist countries. If your country is covered by the agreement you will be allowed to stay in Japan without a visa for between 15 days and six months, depending on the country and your purpose for coming to Japan.

Immigration will stamp your passport and give you a status of residence which specifies how long you can stay. For tourists this is in practice normally three months. If you want to extend your period of stay you must go to an Immigration Office (*Nyukoku Kanri Jimusho*) and fill in a form stating your reason. If the application is accepted you pay a ¥4,000 fee. The address of Tokyo's Immigration Service Center is: World Import Mart Building, 6th Fl. Sunshine City
1-3, Higashi-Ikebukuro 3-chome

Toshima-ku Tokyo
Tel: (03) 986-2271

With a tourist visa you are not allowed to work.

If your country is not covered by a visa exemption agreement, obtain a visa from the Japanese Embassy before you set out.

If you plan to stay in Japan for more than three months you should go to the local municipal office well in advance with two 5 cm. x 5 cm. (2 in. x 2 in.) mug shots and fill in two copies of the Application for Alien Registration form. You will generally be issued with your Alien Registration Certificate (colloquially known as the *Gaijin card*) on the spot. You should carry it with you at all times. Not doing so can mean spending several hours at a police station and writing an apology.

CUSTOMS ALLOWANCES

You may bring three 760 ml. (1-1/3 pints) bottles of alcoholic beverages into Japan with you; also 400 cigarettes or 100 cigars or 500 gm. (1 lb. 1-1/2 oz.) of tobacco, 57 gm. (2 oz.) of perfume, two watches providing their value is less than ¥30,000 each and other goods with a total value of not more than ¥100,000.

Don't try to bring marijuana or other illegal narcotics into the country; the last famous person who tried was Paul McCartney and he spent the whole of his stay behind bars. The Japanese authorities are very strict about drugs. Firearms, too, are strictly controlled.

The Japanese pornography law is curiously tight: don't be too shocked if your copy of Playboy is confiscated.

CURRENCY

You can and should buy some yen as soon as you are through Customs. Rates

fluctuate, of course, but are roughly as follows:

US\$1 = ¥146; ¥1,000 = US\$6.85
£1 = ¥234.48; ¥1,000 = £4.26
DM1 = ¥80.57; ¥1,000 = DM12.41
HK\$1 = ¥18.72; ¥1,000 = HK\$53.42
FF1 = ¥24.2; ¥1,000 = FF41.32
A\$1 = ¥99.21; ¥1,000 = A\$10.08

Yen come in 1-yen, 5-yen, 10-yen, 50-yen, 100-yen and 500-yen coins, and 100-yen, 500-yen, 1,000-yen, 5,000-yen and 10,000-yen notes.

Currencies of the following nations may be changed directly into yen: Australia, Canada, Denmark, England, France, Norway, Switzerland and the USA.

IN FROM NARITA

All agree that Narita is a ludicrous distance from the center of town, and there are several alternative ways to get there.

For many travelers the best way is by the Keisei Railway's Skyliner train. All seats are reserved and tickets should be bought in the airport, opposite the Arrivals gate. A shuttle bus will take you from the airport to Narita Kuko station from where the trains leave. The trains travel non-stop between Narita and Ueno, a few stations north of Tokyo, the journey takes exactly one hour and trains leave every 30 minutes on the hour and half-hour.

A practical alternative to the Skyliner is the very comfortable limousine which runs between the airport and the Tokyo City Air Terminal. The journey takes about 80 minutes, though if traffic is heavy this may be as long as two hours. The main drawback is that the terminal is located in a godforsaken place called Hakozaki and you have to take another bus, of which there are plenty, to Tokyo station.

A third alternative is the bus service which runs between the airport and Tokyo's major hotels. There is a special counter with information about this on the airport's ground floor. This is much the most convenient option for visitors who have made hotel reservations before arrival. Call in at the TIC office on Narita's ground floor, between North and South Wings, for details.

If these complexities incline you to postpone your Japan trip indefinitely you could consider flying China Airlines to Haneda. Not surprisingly, they are well booked up in advance.

ACCOMMODATION

Speaking very broadly, there are four basic types of accommodation in Japan: *ryokan*, major hotels, *bijinesu* (business) hotels and hostels. Prices vary widely. The most expensive *ryokan* in Kyoto may set you back about ¥40,000 per night, while the cheapest *ryokan* in the same city may not even cost ¥4,000. There are many choices available between those extremes, but however much or little you choose to fork out you can be almost certain of cleanliness, honest and prompt service and fine plumbing.

Most of Japan's internationally renowned hotels are concentrated in the capital, and include the **Akasaka Prince** with its brand-new tower, the **Takanawa Prince**, also newly reconstructed, and the famous **Okura** which

is aging very elegantly. Outside Tokyo the **Miyako** in Kyoto and the **Hakone Prince** in Hakone are rightly respected around the world.

Business hotels, marked with a 'ß' in the listing, are a peculiarly Japanese category aimed principally at the many Japanese businessmen traveling around the country on tight budgets. They offer decent, no-frills accommodation often in extremely compact rooms, a large proportion of which are singles (usually charged at no more than half the price of twins.) Though not aimed at foreigners they present no cultural problems -- unless you really feel like sprawling. A special feature is the tiny moulded fibergrass bathroom unit each room in a **bijinesu** is fitted with.

yokan were described in **The Culture of Japan**. A good *ryokan* is undoubtedly the most pleasant way of getting close to Japan. The most opulent ones will amaze, but often the simpler ones are just as nice; simplicity, after all is what so much of the Japanese aes-

thetic sense is about.

Before gasping at the prices charged by some of the *ryokan* listed below, remember that supper and breakfast are as a rule included in the overnight charge. Food is indeed often one of the best things about staying in a *ryokan*; your supper may consist of as many as 20 side dishes in addition to rice and soup.

Japanese youth hostels are like youth hostels all over the world: cheap, well-located, rough-and-ready, over-organized and segregated by sex. There are two types: Japan Youth Hostels, Inc. hostels and public hostels run by local authorities. The latter have no membership requirement. As there are over 500 hostels nationwide, many located in remote and picturesque spots, and some occupying the spare rooms of old temples, they are one of the best bets for the intrepid. If that means you, don't leave Tokyo without a copy of *Youth Hostels in Japan*, a booklet available at the TIC, and the *Japan Youth Hostels Handbook*, on sale at Ichigaya hostel (address and phone number below). The latter is in Japanese but can readily be used by people who don't know the language, with a little initial help from a friend to sort out the symbols. Remember to book well in advance for holiday periods. The following list of accommodation covers the major destinations throughout Japan, listed alphabetically. Broadly speaking, value and convenience of location were the selection criteria. Western style establishments are listed first, followed by *Ryokan*.

Room rate indications are as follows:
Inexpensive: ¥4,000 and under.
Moderate: ¥4,000-10,000.
Average and upward: ¥10,000-20,000.
Expensive: ¥20,000 and upward.

An asterisk (*) denotes an establishment with both Western- and Japanese-style rooms.

WESTERN STYLE ACCOMMODATION (INCLUDING YOUTH HOSTELS)

ASO, Kumamoto Prefecture
Aso Kanko Hotel, Yunotani, Choyo-mura, Aso-gun, tel: (09676) 7-0311. 30 rooms. Rates: average and upward.
Aso Youth Hostel, 922-2, Bochu, Aso-machi, Aso-gun, tel: (09673) 4-0804. 60 beds. Rates: inexpensive.

BEPPU, Oita Prefecture
Beppu Youth Hostel, Kankaiji-onsen, tel: (0977) 23-4116. 150 beds. Rates: inexpensive.
Suginoi Hotel, 2272, Oaza Minami-Tateishi, tel: (0977) 24-1141. 90* rooms. Rates: average and upward.

EIHEIJI (near Fukui)
Eiheiji Monzen Youth Hostel, 22-3, Shihi, Eiheiji-machi, Yoshida-gun, Fukui-ken, tel: (0776) 63-3123. 46 beds. Rates: inexpensive.

ENOSHIMA, Kanagawa Prefecture

Enoshima Grand Hotel, 2-16-6, Kata-sekaigan, Fujisawa, tel: (0466) 26-4111. 26* rooms. Rates: average and upward.

FUKUOKA, Fukuoka Prefecture
Hakata Green Hotelß, 4-4, Hakataeki-Chuo-gai, Hakata-ku, tel: (092) 451-4111. 500 rooms. Rates: moderate.
Mitsui Urban Hotel Fukuokaß, 2-8, Hakata-ekimae, Hakata-ku, tel: (092) 451-5111. 310 rooms. Rates: moderate.

HAKONE, Kanagawa Prefecture
Hakone Prince Hotel, 144, Moto-Hakone, Hakone-machi, tel: (0460) 3-

OPPOSITE Store sign in Takayama. ABOVE Inside the Osaka Capsule Inn. This cheap but uniquely claustrophobic mode of accommodation has spread to every major city in the nation. Rates are under ¥4,000 per night and most are located near major business centers. Many only cater for males. If you insist on trying one, tell the cab driver '*Capseru Hoteru*'.

7111, tx: 3892609 HAKPRI J. 96 rooms. Rates: expensive.

Hakone-Sounzan Youth Hostel, 1320, Gora, Hakone-machi, Ashigarashimo-gun, tel: (0460) 2-3827. 27 beds. Rates: inexpensive.

HIROSHIMA, Hiroshima Prefecture
Hiroshima Tokyu Innß, 3-17, Ko-machi, Naka-ku, tel: (082) 244-0109. 284 rooms. Rates: moderate.
Hiroshima Youth Hostel, 1-13-6, Ushita-shin-machi, Higashi-ku, tel: (082) 221-5343. 104 beds. Rates: inexpensive.

IBUSUKI, Kagoshima Prefecture
Ibusuki Kanko Hotel, 3755, Juni-cho, tel: (09932) 2-2131. 455* rooms. Rates: average and upward.
Ibusuki Youth Hostel, 2-1-20, Yunohama, tel: (09932) 2-2758. 96 beds. Rates: inexpensive.

ISE, Mie Prefecture
Ise-shima Youth Hostel, 1219-80, Anagawa, Isobe-cho, Shima-gun, tel: (05995) 5-0226. 120 beds. Rates: inexpensive.

KAGOSHIMA, Kagoshima Prefecture
Kagoshima Daiichi Hotelß, 1-4-1, Takashi, tel: (0992) 55-7591. 68 rooms. Rates: moderate.
Sakurajima Youth Hostel, Yokoha-ma, Sakurajima-cho, Kagoshima-gun, tel: (099293) 2150. 95 beds. Rates: inexpensive.

KANAZAWA, Ishikawa Prefecture
Castle Inn Kanazawaß, 10-17, Kono-hana-machi, tel: (0762) 23-6300. 100 rooms. Rates: moderate.
Kanazawa Youth Hostel, 37, Sue-hiro-cho, tel: (0762) 52-3414. 120 beds. Rates: inexpensive.

KOBE, Hyogo Prefecture
Oriental Hotel, 25, Kyo-machi, Chuo-ku, tel: (078) 331-8111, tx: 5622327

ORIENT J. 190 rooms. Rates: average and upward.
Kobe Union Hotelß, 2-1-9, Nunobiki-cho, Chuo-ku, tel: (078) 222-6500. 167 rooms. Rates: moderate.
Tarumi Kaigan Youth Hostel, 5-58, Kaigan-dori, Tarumi-ku, tel: (078) 707-2133. 28 beds. Rates: inexpensive.

KUMAMOTO, Kumamoto Prefecture
Kumamoto Daiichi Hotelß, 356, Motoyama-machi, tel: (096) 325-5151. 84 rooms. Rates: moderate.
Kumamoto Hotel Castle, 4-2 Joto-machi, tel: (096) 326-3311, tx: 762747 CASTLE J. 214 rooms. Rates: average and upward.
Kumamoto Shiritsa Youth Hostel, 5-15-55 Shimazaki-machi, tel: (0963) 52-2441, 64 beds. Rates: inexpensive.

KURASHIKI, Okayama Prefecture
Kurashiki Kokusai Hotel, 1-1-44, Chuo, tel: (0864) 22-5141, tx: 5933158 KKHTL J. 70* rooms. Rates: average and upward.
Kurashiki Youth Hostel, 1537-1, Mukaiyama, tel: (0864) 22-7355. 80 beds. Rates: inexpensive.

KYOTO
Higashiyama Youth Hostel, 112, Shirakawabashi-goken-cho, Sanjo-dori, Higashiyama-ku, tel: (075) 761-8135. 112 beds. Rates: inexpensive.
Holiday Inn Kyoto, 36, Nishi-hirakicho, Takano, Sakyo-ku, tel: (075) 721-3131, tx: 5422251 INNKYO J. 270 rooms. Rates: average and upward.
Kyoto Central Innß, Shijo-Kawara-machi-nishi-iru, Shimogyo-ku, tel: (075) 211-1666. 148* rooms. Rates: moderate.
Miyako Hotel, Sanjo Keage, Higashi-yama-ku, tel: (075) 771-7111, tx: 5422132 MIYAKO J. 453* rooms. Rates: average and upward.

MIYAJIMA
Makoto Kaikan Youth Hostel, 756, Sairen-cho, Miyajima-machi, Saiki-gun, tel: (08294) 4-0328. 75 beds. Rates: inexpensive.

MIYAZAKI, Miyazaki Prefecture
Sun Hotel Phoenix, 3083, Hamayama, Shioji, Miyazaki City 880-01, tel: (0985) 39-3131, tx: 777859 PHENIX J. 204* rooms. Rates: average and upward.
Aoshima Youth Hostel, 130, Umizoi, Oriuzaka, tel: (0985) 65-1657, 100 beds.

NAGASAKI, Nagasaki Prefecture
Business Hotel Dejimaß, 2-13, Dejima-machi, tel: (0958) 24-7141. 44 rooms. Rates: inexpensive.
Nagasaki Grand Hotel, 5-3, Manzai-machi, tel: (0958) 23-1234. 126* rooms. Rates: average and upward.
Nagasaki Oranda-Zaka Youth Hostel, 6-14, Higashi-yamate-cho, tel: (0958) 22-2730. 55 beds. Rates: inexpensive.

NAGOYA, Aichi Prefecture
Nagoya Kanko Hotel, 1-19-30, Nishiki, Naka-ku, tel: (052) 231-7711, tx: 59946 KANHO J. 505 rooms. Rates: average and upward.
Nagoya Green Hotelß, 1-8-22, Nishiki, Naka-ku, tel: (052) 203-0211. 105 rooms. Rates: moderate.
Nagoya Youth Hostel, 1-50, Kameiri, Tashiro-cho, Chikusa-ku, tel: (052) 781-9845. 100 beds. Rates: inexpensive.

NAHA, Okinawa Prefecture
Naha Youth Hostel, 51, Onoyama-cho, tel: (0988) 57-0073. 100 beds. Rates: Inexpensive.
Okinawa Hotel, 35, Daido, tel: (0988) 84-3191. 65* rooms. Rates: average and upward.
Okinawa Miyako Hotel, 40, Matsukawa, tel: (0988) 87-1111. 318 rooms. Rates: average and upward.

NARA, Nara Prefecture
Nara Hotel, 1096, Takabatake-cho, tel: (0742) 26-3300, tx: 5522108 NARAHO J. 132* rooms. Rates: average and upward.
Hotel Sun Route Naraß, 1110, Takabatake-Bodai-cho, tel: (0742) 22-5151. 95 rooms. Rates: moderate.
Nara Youth Hostel, Sogo-undo-koen, 64, Handa-hiraki-cho, tel: (0742) 22-1334. 120 beds. Rates: inexpensive.

NARITA, Chiba Prefecture
Holiday Inn Narita, 320-1, Tokko, Narita, tel: (0476) 32-1234, tx: 3762133 HIHTL J. 254* rooms. Rates: average and upward.

NIIGATA, Niigata Prefecture
Okura Hotel Niigata, 6-53, Kawabatacho, tel: (0252) 24-6111, tx: 3122815 OKRNIT J. 303* rooms. Rates: average and upward.

NIKKO, Tochigi Prefecture
Nikko Kanaya Hotel, 1300, Kami-Hatsuishi. tel: (0288) 54-0001, tx: 3544451 KANAYA J. 83 rooms. Rates: average and upward.
Nikko Youth Hostel, 1140, Tokorono, tel: (0288) 54-1013. 50 beds. Rates: inexpensive.
Pension Turtleß, 2-16, Takumi-cho, tel: (0288) 53-3168. 6* rooms. Rates: inexpensive.

OSAKA, Osaka Prefecture
Hotel New Hankyu, 1-1-35, Shibata, Kita-ku, tel: (06) 372-5101, tx: 5233830 HTLNH J. 1,020* rooms. Rates: average and upward.
Osaka Dai-ichi Hotel, 1-9-20, Umeda, Kita-ku, tel: (06) 341-4411, tx: 5234423 ITIHLO J. 478 rooms. Rates: average and upward.
Mitsui Urban Hotelß, 3-18-8, Toyosaki, Oyodo-ku, tel: (06) 374-1111. 410 rooms. Rates: moderate.
Osaka Tokyu Innß, 2-1, Doyama-cho, Kita-ku, tel: (06) 315-0109. 402 rooms.

Rates: moderate.
Osaka-Shiritsu Nagai Youth Hostel,
450, Higahsi-nagai-cho, Higashi-sumi-yoshi-ku, tel: (06) 699-5631. 108 beds.
Rates: inexpensive.

SAPPORO, Hokkaido
Sapporo Prince Hotel, 11, Nishi, Minami-Nijo Chuo-ku, tel: (011) 241-1111, tx: 933949 SAPPRI J. 227* rooms. Rates: average and upward.
Sapporo House Youth Hostel, 3-1, Nishi 6-chome, Kita Rokujo, Kita-ku, tel: (011) 721-4235. 124 beds. Rates: inexpensive.
ANA Hotel Sapporo, 1, Nishi-kita-3, Chuo-ku, tel: (011) 221-4411, tx: 934-712 SZENHL J. (SENDAI). 470 rooms. Rates: moderate.

SENDAI, Miyagi Prefecture
Chitose Youth Hostel, 6-3-8, Oda-wara, tel: (0222) 22-6329. 70 beds. Rates: inexpensive.
Hotel Sendai Plaza, 2-20-1 Honcho, tel: (0222) 62-7111, tx: 852-965 PLAZA J. 201 rooms. Rates: moderate.
Sendai Royal Hotelß, 4-10-11, Chuo, tel: (0222) 27-6131. 70 rooms. Rates: moderate.

TAKAMATSU, Kagawa Prefecture
Takamatsu International Hotel, 2191, Kitacho, tel: (0878) 31-1511. 105* rooms. Rates: average and upward.

TAKAYAMA, Gifu Prefecture
Hida Hotel Plaza, 2-60, Hanaokacho, Takayama, tel: (0577) 33-4600. 100* rooms. Rates: average and upward.

TOBA, Mie Prefecture
Toba Hotel International, 1-23-1, Toba, tel: (0599) 25-3121, tx: 4973789 TOBAHL J. 124* rooms. Rates: average and upward.

TOKYO
Akasaka Prince Hotel, 1, Kioi-cho, Chiyoda-ku, tel: (03) 234-1111. 761*

rooms. Rates: average and upward.
Asia Center of Japan, 8-10-32, Akasaka, Minato-ku, tel: (03) 402-6111. 177 rooms. Rates: moderate.
Hotel Ginza Daieiß, 3-12-2, Ginza, Chuo-ku, tel: (03) 541-2681. 97 rooms. Rates: moderate.
Hotel Okura, 2-10-4, Toranomon, Minato-ku, tel: (03) 582-0111, tx: 22790 HTLOKURA J 913* rooms. Rates: expensive.
Hotel Sun Route Shibuyaß, 1-11, Nampeidai, Shibuya-ku, tel: (03) 464-6411. 180 rooms. Rates: moderate.
Tokyo International Youth Hostel, 18th Floor, Central Plaza, 21-1, Kagu-rakashi, Shinjuku-ku, tel: (03) 235-1107. 138 beds. Rates: inexpensive.
Imperial Hotel, 1-1-1, Uchisaiwai-cho, Chiyoda-ku, tel: (03) 504-1111, tx: 222-2346 IMPHO J. 1,125 rooms. Rates: expensive.
Okubo House (Hostel), 1-11-32,, Hyakunin-cho, Shinjuku-ku, tel: (03) 361-2348. 11* rooms (bunk beds). Rates: inexpensive.
Taisho Central Hotelß, 1-27-7, Taka-danobaba, Shinjuku-ku, tel: (03) 232-0101. 200 rooms. Rates: moderate.
Takanawa Prince Hotel, 3-13-1, Takanawa, Minato-ku, tel: (03) 447-1111, tx: 242-3232 TAKPRH J. 400* rooms. Rates: average and upward.
The New Otani, 4, Kioi-cho, Chiyoda-ku, tel: (03) 265-1111, tx: 24719 HTLOTANI J. 2,051 rooms. Rates: average and upward.
Toko Hotelß, 2-6-8, Nishi-Gotanda, Shinagawa-ku, tel: (03) 494-1050. 337 rooms. Rates: moderate.
Tokyo Yoyogi Youth Hostel, 3-1, Yoyogi-kamizono, Shibuya-ku, tel: (03) 467-9163. 150 beds. Rates: inexpensive.
Ueno Station Hotelß, 2-14-23, Ueno, Taito-ku, tel: (03) 833-5111. 85* rooms. Rates: moderate.

YOKOHAMA, Kanagawa Prefecture
Bund Hotel, 1-2-14, Shin-Yamashita, Naka-ku, tel: (045) 621-1101. 50*

rooms. Rates: average and upward.
Hotel Aster, 87, Yamashitacho, Naka-ku, tel: (045) 651-0141. 72* rooms. Rates: average and upward.
Yokohama Portside Hotelß, 3-95, Hanasakicho, Naka-ku, tel: (045) 242-4411. 77 rooms. Rates: moderate.

RYOKAN

ASO, Kamamoto Prefecture
Aso Kanko Hotel, Yunotani, Choyo-mura, Aso-gun, tel: (09676) 7-0311. 60* rooms. Rates: average and upward.
Asonotsukasa, 1197, Matsunoki, Oaza Kurogawa, Aso-machi, Aso-gun, tel: (09673) 4-0811. 63 rooms. Rates: average and upward.

BEPPU, Oita Prefecture
Hotel Shin-Nogami, 1-8-8, Kitahama, tel: (0977) 23-2141. 31 rooms. Rates: average and upward.
Shohaso, 14-32, Shohaen-machi, tel: (0977) 66-0013. 10 rooms. Rates: moderate.
Suginoi Hotel, 2272, Oaza Minami-Tateishi, tel: (0977) 24-1141. 510* rooms. Rates: average and upward.

ENOSHIMA, Kanagawa Prefecture
Iwamotoro Bekkan (Enoshima Grand Hotel), 2-16-6, Katasekaigan, Fujisawa, tel: (0466) 26-4111. 27* rooms. Rates: average and upward.

FUJI-GO-KO (Fuji Five Lakes District), Yamanashi Prefecture
Hotel Bugaku-so, 508, Hirano, Yama-nakako-mura, Minami-Tsuru-gun, tel: (0555) 62-1100. 24 rooms. Rates: moderate.
Hotel Hyakkei-en, 51-1, Azagawa, Kawaguchiko-machi, Minami-Tsuru-gun, tel: (05557) 2-0554. 20 rooms. Rates: moderate.

HAKONE, Kanagawa Prefecture
Hotel Yamadaya, 1320, Gora, Hakone-machi, Ashigara-Shimo-gun, tel: (0460)

2-2641. 16 rooms. Rates: average and upward.
Matsuzaka-ya, 64, Moto-Hakone, Hakone-machi, Ashigara-Shimo-gun, tel: (0460) 3-6315. 20 rooms. Rates: average and upward.
Naraya Ryokan, 162, Miyanoshita, Hakone-machi, Ashigara-shimo-gun, tel: (0460) 2-2411. 25 rooms. Rates: expensive.
Suizanso, 694, Yumoto, Hakone-machi, Ashigara-shimo-gun, tel: (0460) 5-5757. 26 rooms. Rates: average and upward.

HIROSHIMA, Hiroshima Prefecture
Kumano Ryokan, 11-6, Kawaramachi, Naka-ku, tel: (082) 231-4890. 14 rooms. Rates: moderate.

IBUSUKI, Kagoshima Prefecture
Ibusuki Kanko Hotel, 3755, Junicho, tel: (09932) 2-2131. 167* rooms. Rates: average and upward.

ISE, Mie Prefecture
Saekikan, 6-4, Hom-machi, tel: (0596) 28-2017. 29 rooms. Rates: average and upward.

KANAZAWA, Ishikawa Prefecture
Chaya Ryokan, 2-17-21, Hommachi, tel: (0762) 31-2225. 24 rooms. Rates: moderate.
Ryumeikan, 39-2, Nishicho-Yabunou-chi, tel: (0762) 63-8444. 12 rooms. Rates: moderate.

KOBE, Hyogo Prefecture
Hotel Kobe, 5-2-31, Kumochi-cho, Chuo-ku, tel: (078) 221-5431. 43 rooms. Rates: average and upward.
Ryokan Takayamaso, 400-1, Arima-cho, Kita-ku, tel: (078) 904-0744. 21 rooms. Rates: average and upward.

KUMAMOTO, Kumamoto Prefecture
Hotel Takeya, 2-7-1, Kyo-machi, tel: (096) 325-6840. 12 rooms. Rates: moderate.

KYOTO

Chigiriya Ryokan, Takoyakushi-dori-Tominokoji-nishi-iru, Nakagyo-ku, tel: (075) 221-1281. 45 rooms. Rates: average and upward.

Izumiya Ryokan, Nishi-Nakasuji, Shomen-sagaru, Shimogyo-ku, tel: (075) 371-2769. 18 rooms. Rates: moderate.

Kaneiwaro Bekkan, Kiyamachi-dori-Matsubara-sagaru, Shimogyo-ku, tel: (075) 351-5010. 23 rooms. Rates: average and upward.

Matsubaya Ryokan, Kamijuzuya-machi-dori, Higashinotoin-nishi-iru, Shimogyo-ku, tel: (075) 351-3727. 11 rooms. Rates: inexpensive.

Matsukichi Ryokan, Goko-machi, Sanjo-agaru, Nakagyo-ku, tel: (075) 221-7016. 15 rooms. Rates: expensive.

Miyako Hotel, Sanjo Keage, Higashiyama-ku, tel: (075) 771-7111, tx: 5422132 MIYAKO J. 27* rooms. Rates: expensive.

Ryokan Hiraiwa, Ninomiya-machi-dori, Kaminokuchi-agaru, Shimogyo-ku, tel: (075) 351-6748. 16 rooms. Rates: inexpensive.

Ryokan Shichijo-so, 7, Ikkyo-Miya-nouchicho, Higashiyama-ku, tel: (075) 561-9796. 10 rooms. Rates: inexpensive.

Sumiya Ryokan, Fuyacho-dori, Sanjo-sagaru, Nakagyo-ku, tel: (075) 221-2188. 26 rooms. Rates: expensive.

Tani House, 8, Daitokuji-cho, Murasakino, Kita-ku, tel: (075) 492-5489. 10 rooms. Rates: inexpensive.

Traditional Inn Wakazuru, 50, Shimogamo, Izumigawa-cho, Sakyo-ku, tel: (075) 711-1131. 15 rooms. Rates: moderate.

MIYAJIMA.

Kamefuku, 849, Miyajima-cho, Saeki-gun, tel: (0829) 44-2111. 43 rooms. Rates: expensive.

MIYAZAKI

Sun Hotel Phoenix, 3083, Hamayama, Shioji, Miyazaki City, tel: (0985) 39-3131, tx: 777859 PHENIX J. 96* rooms. Rates: average and upward.

NAGASAKI, Nagasaki Prefecture

Korakuso, 2-4, Yoriai-machi, tel: (0958) 21-2584. 21 rooms. Rates: moderate.

NAGOYA, Aichi Prefecture

Maizurukan, 1-18-24, Meikei-minami, Nakamura-ku, tel: (052) 541-1346. 23 rooms. Rates: average and upward.

Satsuki Honten, 1-18-30, Meieki-Minami, Nakamura-ku, tel: (052) 551-0052. 10 rooms. Rates: moderate.

NAHA, Okinawa Prefecture

Okinawa Hotel, 35, Daido, tel: (0988) 84-3191. 13* rooms. Rates: average and upward.

NARA, Nara Prefecture

Kasuga Hotel, 40-4, Noborioji-cho, tel: (0742) 22-4031. 44 rooms. Rates: average and upward.

Ryokan Seikanso, 29, Higashi-Kitsuji-cho, tel: (0742) 22-2670. 12 rooms. Rates: inexpensive.

NARITA, Chiba Prefecture

Business Hotel Tsukuba, 847, Hanasaki-cho, tel: (0476) 24-1234. 15 rooms. Rates: moderate.

Ohgiya, 474, Saiwai-cho, tel: (0476) 22-1161. 30 rooms. Rates: moderate.

NIIGATA, Niigata Prefecture

Onoya Ryokan, 981, Furumachi-dori, Rokuban-cho, tel: (0252) 29-2951. 24 rooms. Rates: average and upward.

NIKKO, Tochigi Prefecture

Chuzenji Hotel, 2478, Chugushi, Nikko, tel: (0288) 55-0333. 121 rooms. Rates: average and upward.

Konishi Bekkan, 1115, Kami-Kachiishi-cho, tel: (0288) 54-1105, 24 rooms. Rates: average and upward.

Nikko Green Hotel, 9-19, Honcho, tel: (0286) 54-1756. 32 rooms. Rates: average and upward.

OSAKA, Osaka Prefecture
Ebisuso Ryokan, 1-7-33, Nihombashi-Nishi, Naniwa-ku, tel: (06) 643-4861. 17 rooms. Rates: inexpensive.

SAPPORO, Hokkaido
Nakamuraya, 1, Nishi-7-chome, Kita-Sanjo, Chuo-ku, tel: (011) 241-2111. 26 rooms. Rates: moderate.

SENDAI, Miyagi Prefecture
Ryokan Kurihara, 2-1-27, Kakyoin, tel: (0222) 22-5076. 22 rooms. Rates: moderate.

TAKAMATSU, Kagawa Prefecture
Tokiwa Honkan, 1-8-2, Tokiwacho, tel: (0878) 61-5577. 22 rooms. Rates: average and upward.

TAKAYAMA, Gifu Prefecture
Hida Hotel, 2-60, Hanaoka-cho, Taka-yama, tel: (0577) 33-4600. 55* rooms. Rates: average and upward.
Ryokan Seiryu 6, Hanakawa-machi, Takayama, tel: (0577) 32-0448. 24 rooms. Rates: average and upward.

TOBA, Mie Prefecture
Kimpokan, 1-10-38, Toba, tel: (0599) 25-2001. 50 rooms. Rates: average and upward.
Toba Kokusai Hotel Wafu Bekkan, 1-23-1, Toba, tel: (0599) 25-3121. 45 rooms. Rates: average and upward.

TOKYO
English House, 2-23-8, Nishi-Ikebu-kuro, Toshima-ku, tel: (03) 988-1743. 15 rooms. Rates: inexpensive.
Fukudaya, 6-12, Kioi-cho, Chiyoda-ku, tel: (03) 261-8577. 13 rooms. Rates: expensive.
Hotel Okura, 2-10-4, Toranomon, Minato-ku, tel: (03) 582-0111, tx: 22790 HTLOKURA J. 11* rooms. Rates: expensive.
Inabaso, 5-6-13, Shinjuku, Shinjuku-ku, tel: (03) 341-9581. 11 rooms. Rates: moderate.
Mickey House, 2-15-1, Nakadai, Ita-bashi-ku, tel: (03) 936-8889. 15 rooms. Rates: inexpensive.
Okubo House, 1-11-32, Hyakunin-cho, Shinjuku-ku, tel: (03) 361-2348. 18* rooms. Rates: inexpensive.
Ryokan Chomeikan, 4-4-8, Hongo, Bunkyo-ku, tel: (03) 811-7205. 27 rooms. Rates: moderate.
Ryokan Mikawaya Bekkan, 1-31-11, Asakusa, Taito-ku, tel: (03) 843-2345. 12 rooms. Rates: moderate.
Sansuiso Ryokan, 2-9-5, Higashi-Go-tanda, Shinagawa-ku, tel: (03) 441-7475. 9 rooms. Rates: inexpensive.
Shinkomatsu, 1-9-13, Tsukiji, Chuo-ku, tel: (03) 541-2225. 10 rooms. Rates: average and upward.
Takanawa Prince Hotel, 3-13-1, Takanawa, Minato-ku, tel: (03) 447-1111, tx: 242-3232 TAKPRH J. 18* rooms. Rates: expensive.
Ueno Station Hotel, 2-14-23, Ueno, Taito-ku, tel: (03) 833-5111. 15* rooms. Rates: moderate.

YOKOHAMA, Kanagawa Prefecture
Yamashiroya Ryokan, 2-159, Hinode-cho, Naka-ku, tel: (045) 231-1146. 10 rooms. Rates: moderate.

THE ROVING GOURMET

While traveling around Japan there is no need to put up with inferior food. Restaurants of a decent standard are to be found in almost every town of any size. Furthermore, many towns and cities have their *meibutsu*, the product or dish for which that particular area is renowned, and discovering and sampling these can lend an extra dimension of adventure to your journey. Below are listed representative restaurants in 25 towns and cities throughout the country, together with their phone numbers and, in cases where it was possible to determine it, a figure suggesting roughly what a meal for one will cost.

'Course' (Japanese '*kosu*') means a

full set meal. Ordering a la carte, it is usually possible to eat more cheaply than the course price suggests.

Unless you speak Japanese the easiest way to use the list below is to get a Japanese person to call the restaurant in question -- maybe your hotel clerk -- to make a reservation (if this is necessary or possible) and obtain directions.

BEPPU
Marukiyo, tel: (0979) 22-4055. Fish, including *fugu* (blowfish).

FUKUOKA
Shizuka, tel: (092) 712-4500. This is

the best part of the country for *fugu* (blowfish) and Shizuka is a *fugu* specialist. ¥3,500 up.
Suigetsu, tel: (092) 411-9501. *Nabe* (Japanese-style stew) specialty. Course ¥5,000 up.

HIROSHIMA
Chez Yamarai, tel: (0822) 94-1200. French-style food, including oysters. ¥3,500 up.
Kakifune-Kanawa, tel: (0822) 41-7416. Japanese-style. Special course ¥8,000 up.

ISE (Ise-shi)
Tekonejaya, tel: (0596) 22-3384. *Sushi* and *sashimi*.
(Kashikojima)
Shima Kanko Hotel, tel: (05994)

3-1211. Famous for French cuisine and lobster dishes. ¥6,000 and up.

KAGOSHIMA
Nagura, tel: (09937) 2-5026. *Katsuo* (bonito sashimi) and other dishes. ¥1,500 up.
Satsuma-ji, tel: (0992) 26-0525. Traditional local *satsuma ryori* cuisine. ¥3,500 up.

KANAZAWA
Kanazawa, tel: (0762) 23-4439. *Robata-yaki.*

KAMAKURA
Monzen, tel: (0467) 25-1121. In this town of Zen temples. *shojin ryori*, the elaborate vegetarian temple cuisine, is the special (though expensive) treat. *Monzen* means 'outside the gate', and it is indeed just outside the gate of Enkakuji in Kita-Kamakura, one of the town's most august monasteries. *Shojin ryori*, ¥2,200 up; the elaborate *kaiseki ryori* ¥3,000 up.

KOBE
Aotatsu, tel: (078) 331 3435. *Sushi*; *anago* (conger eel) a speciality. Course ¥1,600 up.

KUMAMOTO
Dengaku-ya, tel: (0963) 29 8011. *Dengaku* (broiled *tofu*) and other dishes.
Tagosaku, tel: (0963) 53-4171. Country-style Japanese food, including horsemeat *sashimi*, a local specialty. ¥3,500 up.

KYOTO
Daimonjiya, tel: (075) 221-0605. The speciality is elaborate and beautiful *bento* (lunch boxes) eaten on the premises. ¥3,000 up.
Daitokuji Monzen, which means 'in front of the gate of Daitokuji Temple', tel: (075) 493-0019. *Shojin ryori*. ¥5,000 up.

Restaurants in ABOVE Tokyo, OPPOSITE, TOP Takayama, BOTTOM LEFT Osaka and BOTTOM RIGHT Yokohama.

MATSUMOTO

Furusato, tel: (0263) 33-3717. *Soba* (buckwheat noodles) shop. ¥500 up.
Mikawa-ya, tel: (0263) 32-0339. *Basashi* (horsemeat *sashimi*), ¥1,800 up.

MIYAZAKI

Sato (Miyazaki Kanko Hotel), tel: (0985) 27-1212. *Sashimi*, including very rare mushroom *sashimi*.
Zushi-Shokudo, tel: (0985) 67-0122. Lobster specialist. ¥2,000 up.

NAGASAKI

Fukudaya, tel: (0957) 22-0101. *Unagi* (broiled eel). ¥800 up.
Shikaire, tel: (0958) 22-1296. Nagasaki *chanpon* local Chinese-style noodles. ¥500 up.

NAGOYA

Gomitori, tel: (052) 241-0041. Loaches, frogs, spare ribs. ¥1,500 up.
Kishimen Tei, tel: (052) 951-3481.

Kishimen or flat white noodles, are a speciality of Nagoya, and this is a good place to sample them. ¥500 up.
Torikyu, tel: (052) 541-2747. High-class *yakitoriya*. Course ¥4,000 up.

NAHA

Hanazumi, tel: (098998) 67-3972. Okinawa specialities. Course ¥5,000.
Naha, tel: (098998) 68-2548. Local specialities, including pig's trotters and goat. Course ¥5,000 up.

NARA

Tonochaya, tel: (0742) 22-4348.
Chameshi (dishes with rice cooked in tea) specialist inside Kofukuji Temple. Also *somen* (Japanese vermicelli, a Nara *meibutsu*). *Chameshi* set ¥2,000 up.

NIKKO

Kanaya Hotel, tel: (0288) 54-0001. Elegant old hotel specializing in trout dishes (*nijimasu*). ¥2,800 up.

OKAYAMA

Shihoya, tel: (0862) 24-5495. Fish restaurant; *tai* (sea bream) a speciality. Course ¥4,000 up.

OSAKA

Imai, tel: (06) 211-0319. *Udon* house in famous Dotonbori area. ¥350 up.
Itoya, tel: (06) 341-2891. *Okonomiyaki*, delicious -- and cheap -- do-it-yourself omelette-cum-pancake. ¥500 up.

SAPPORO

Beeru-en, tel: (011) 742-1531. Steak and lamb dishes ('Genghis Khan') in converted nineteenth-century brewery. ¥3,000 up.
Kanikke, tel: (011) 231-4080. *Kani* (crab) dishes. ¥2,000 up.
Taisei, tel: (011) 251-6821. Hokkaido fish dishes. including *nabe* (stew-like) style. ¥1,500 up.

SENDAI

Kaitoku, tel: (0222) 22-0785. Oyster

Nara temple restaurant offering winter fare, including *oden*.

dishes. Course ¥4,000 up.

TAKAMATSU
Hamasaku, tel: (0878) 21-6044. Fish *tempura*-style. ¥700 up.

TAKAYAMA
Suzuya, tel: (0577) 32-2484. *Sansai* (wild mushroom vegetables), beef, *hoba* (special local *miso* cooked on a leaf).

TOKUSHIMA
Saijo, tel: (0886) 95-2775. *Udon* (fat white noodles) are the speciality of Shikoku. Here they serve *tarai udon*, literally 'bathtub *udon*' in wooden bathtub-shaped dishes. ¥400 up.

YUMOTO
Hatsuhana, tel: (0460) 5-8287. *Soba* (buckwheat noodles) specialist.

TOURIST INFORMATION

Phone numbers of Japan's three Tourist Information Centers (TICs) are as follows:
Tokyo (near Yurakucho and Hibiya stations): (03) 502-1461

Narita Airport: (0476) 32-8711

Kyoto (Kyoto Tower Building, near Kyoto station): (075)371-5649

All three offices are open from 9 a.m. to 5 p.m. Monday to Friday and 9 a.m. to noon on Saturdays. They are closed on Sundays and national holidays.

The TIC's staff are well aware that there are not nearly enough branches to deal with the large numbers of foreign tourists coming to Japan these days, but they work hard to make up for it and go to a lot of trouble to be helpful. They will give you maps, leaflets, guides and help you with travel schedules. One of the best things they've done is to pre-

pare a series of mini-guides, leaflets full of detailed, practical and up-to-date information about how to get the most out of your trip to a large number of popular destinations in the country. These are not on the shelves in TIC offices; you have to ask for the particular guide or guides you need.

The following is a list of mini-guides currently available:

Karuizawa Kogen
Izu Peninsula
Sendai, Matsushima and Vicinity
Chichibu
Okutama
Kamakura
Hakone
Fuji Five Lakes
Climbing Mt. Fuji
Walking Tour Courses in Kyoto
Annual Events in Japan
Reasonable Accommodation in Japan
Nikko
Narita
Matsumoto and Kamikochi
Takayama and Vicinity
Walking Tour Courses in Nara
Ise-shima
Hiroshima and Miyajima
Museums and Art Galleries
Ceramics
Traditional Sports
Skiing in Japan
Japan Alps
Sapporo and Vicinity
Nagoya and Vicinity
Inland Sea National Park
Beppu, Aso and Kumamoto
Nagasaki and Unzen
Japanese Gardens
Towada-Hachimantai National Park
Kanazawa and Noto Peninsula
Walking Tour Courses in Tokyo
Matsue and Isumo-Taisha Shrine
Fukuoka
Southern Kyushu

If you need travel advice in English and you can't get to a TIC office, call

191

them. Outside Tokyo and Kyoto you can take advantage of the free Japan Travel-Phone service. Dial 106 and tell the operator, in English, 'Collect Call TIC'. Remember to speak slowly and clearly. You can use this service from a private phone or from a yellow or blue public phone, but not from a red one. If calling from a public phone, insert a ten-yen coin before you dial. It will be returned to you when you replace the receiver.

The TIC will help you in any way they can, but they make the point that they are not a travel agency. So don't expect them to make, for example, hotel reservations for you. If they are not too busy, however, and if it is likely that the person on the other end won't understand English, they will go with you to a public phone in the office and help you out with your call. Travel Nippon, mentioned under **minshuku** above, have English-speaking staff and will make reservations for you.

WEIGHTS AND MEASURES

Metric, centigrade. A few old measures -- *i-sho*, about half a gallon, used for sake, and *tsubo*, the area of two *tatami* mats, used for measuring the area of land -- add some spice.

COMMUNICATIONS

TELEPHONES

You will probably be startled by the number of public telephones in Japan, both in Tokyo and elsewhere. Many of them are just there on the street, quite unprotected; almost all of them work. They come in five colors: pink, red, blue, yellow and green. Pink ones take only 10-yen coins. Some red and blue and all yellow and green ones take 100-yen coins as well. Green ones also

accept special cards.

They're easy to use. Lift the receiver, insert one or more coins and dial. Have the number handy and dial promptly or you will have to start all over again. To avoid being cut off in midstream it is a good idea to put a few coins in at the start: some red phones will accept six 10-yen coins, others will accept five 10-yen and four 100-yen coins, and when you've finished they will return coins which have not been used. They will not, however, return fractions of 100-yen coins unused. Within the city you get three minutes' talking time for 10 yen. When dialing a Tokyo number from outside the city, prefix the number with 03. To get the overseas operator dial 0051.

POST OFFICES

They are called *yubin-kyoku* and function in the normal manner. The symbol of the post office is ₸. Airmail rates are as follows:

Letter up to 10 g. (1/2 oz)
Asia, Australasia: ¥130
North and Central America: ¥150
Europe, South America, Middle East: ¥170

Postcard
Asia, Australasia: ¥90
North and Central America: ¥100
Europe, South America, Middle East: ¥110

The nearest post office to Tokyo's TIC is in the back of the American Pharmacy, just 50 meters away.

NEWSPAPERS, ETC.

As many as four daily English-language newspapers are available in Tokyo, which is extraordinary considering that native English speakers constitute a tiny minority. The *Japan Times* (¥140), the Oldest and most famous, is phenomenally dull. The *Mainichi Daily*

News (¥120), and the *Asahi Evening News* (¥120), both offshoots of Japanese-language papers, are more absorbing and print translations of articles from the vernacular press that can be interesting. The *Daily Yomiuri* is only ¥40 but it is very thin.

Apart from *Tour Companion*, the free weekly mentioned earlier, there are a couple of other worthwhile English-language periodicals. The monthly *Tokyo Journal*, ¥500, is the best source of information in English about what's on in town, including concerts and out-of-the-way cinemas and theaters. The weekly *Tokyo Weekender*, free, is aimed more at local residents and servicemen than tourists but has film listings and the odd amusing article.

International magazines and papers are to be found at bookstores in major hotels. These are also the best places to find English-language books about Japan. The Imperial Hotel and New Otani Hotel are among those with good bookstores.

LIBRARIES

Or you may prefer to borrow a book. There are a few good libraries in town where you can borrow books free:

American Center
ABC Kaikan, 2-6-3 Shiba-koen Minato-ku, Tokyo. Tel: (03) 436-0901

This library is stronger on American periodicals than books. Close to Shiba-koen subway station, Toei-Mita line.

British Council
Kenkyusha Eigo Center Building, 1-2 Kagurazaka, Shinjuku-ku, Tokyo, Tel: 03-235-2031

A large library with a British bias. Five minutes' walk from Iidabashi JNR Station (West Exit) and subway station (Exit B3) towards Yotsuya.

The Japan Foundation
Park Building, 3 Kioi-cho, Chiyoda-ku, Tokyo. Tel: (03) 263-4505

The Japan Foundation is Japan's culture-exporting body, modeled on the British Council. It has a good library of books on many Japanese subjects and a quiet reading-room. When you apply for a card it may be as well to say you are studying some aspect of the culture, however informally. Ten minutes from Akasaka-Mitsuke station, past the New Otani Hotel. Phone for directions.

TELEVISION

Then, of course, there's the tube. There are seven regular TV channels available in Tokyo. Almost all broadcasting is in Japanese and most films are dubbed; one of the piquant pleasures of Japan is listening to John Wayne or Charles Bronson speaking fluent Japanese. However, if you can lay hands on a set with *multiplex* you can listen to certain programs, including several news broadcasts and some American soap operas, in English. Details in daily papers and *Tour Companion*.

Major hotels have cable TV and Channel 2 is in English. There are programs morning and evening. See *Tour Companion* for details.

EMBASSIES

Tokyo's embassies are open five days a week. The following are their telephone numbers:

Afghanistan (03) 407-7900
Algeria (03) 711-2661
Argentina (03) 592-0321
Australia (03) 453-0251
Austria (03) 451-8281
Bangladesh (03) 442-1501
Belgium (03) 262-0191
Bolivia (03) 499-5441
Brazil (03) 404-5211
Bulgaria (03) 465-1021

Burma (03) 441-9291
Canada (03) 408-2101
China (03) 403-3380
Chile (03) 452-7561
Colombia (03) 440-6451
Costa Rica (03) 486-1812
Cuba (03) 449-7511
Czechoslovakia (03) 400-8122
Denmark (03) 496-3001
Dominican Republic (03) 499-6020
East Germany (03) 585-5404
Ecuador (03) 499-2800
Egypt (03) 463-4564
El Salvador (03) 499-4461
Ethiopia (03) 585-3151
Finland (03) 442-2231
France (03) 473-0171
Gabon (03) 409-5119
Ghana (03) 409-3861
Greece (03) 403-0871
Guatemala (03) 400-1820
Guinea (03) 499-3281
Haiti (03) 486-7070
Holy See (03) 263-6851
Honduras (03) 409-1150
Hungary (03) 476-6061
India (03) 262-2391
Indonesia (03) 441-4201
Iran (03) 446-8011
Iraq (03) 423-1727
Ireland (03) 263-0695
Israel (03) 264-0911
Italy (03) 453-5291
Ivory Coast (03) 499-7021
Jordan (03) 580-5856
Kenya (03) 479-4006
Republic of Korea (03) 452-7611
Kuwait (03) 455-0361
Laos (03) 408-1166
Lebanon (03) 580-1227
Liberia (03) 499-2451
Libya (03) 477-0701
Madagascar (03) 446-7252
Malaysia (03) 463-0241
Mexico (03) 581-1131
Mongolia (03) 469-2088
Morocco (03) 478-3271
Nepal (03) 444-7303
Netherlands (03) 431-5126
New Zealand (03) 467-2271

Nicaragua (03) 499-0400
Nigeria (03) 468-5531
Norway (03) 440-2611
Oman (03) 402-0877
Pakistan (03) 454-4861
Panama (03) 499-3741
Papua New Guinea (03) 454-7801
Paraguay (03) 447-7496
Peru (03) 406-4240
Philippines (03) 496-2731
Poland (03) 711-5224
Portugal (03) 400-7907
Qatar (03) 446-7561
Romania (03) 479-0311
Rwanda (03) 490-6811
Saudi Arabia (03) 589-5241
Senegal (03) 464-8451
Singapore (03) 586-9111
Spain (03) 583-8531
Sri Lanka (03) 585-7431
Sudan (03) 406-0811
Sweden (03) 582-6981
Switzerland (03) 473-0121
Syria (03) 586-8977
Tanzania (03) 425-4531
Thailand (03) 441-7352
Tunisia (03) 353-4111
Turkey (03) 470-5131
Uganda (03) 469-3641
United Arab Emirates (03) 478-0659
United Kingdom (03) 265-5511
United States (03) 583-7141
Uruguay (03) 486-1888
Union of Soviet Socialist Republics (03) 583-4224
Venezuela (03) 409-1501
Viet Nam (03) 466-3311
West Germany (03) 473-0151
Yemen (03) 499-7151
Yugoslavia (03) 447-3571
Zaire, (03) 406-4981
Zambia (03) 445-1041
European Economic Community Delegation (03) 239-0441

RELIGION

Check weekend issues of the *Japan Times* and back pages of the weekly

Tokyo Weekender for details of Christian and other regular services. Tokyo has a mosque and a synagogue as well as a large number of churches. For Zen meditation, yoga, etc. check the announcements column on the back page of the *Japan Times*.

HEALTH

Avoid getting sick in Japan if you can. Foreigners can join the health insurance system but it's only worthwhile if you are staying a longish time. And if you're not insured you must pay the full cost of pretty hefty medical charges.

Medical treatment is a problem in Japan. Doctors and hospitals with conditions of immaculate hygiene are plentiful, but many doctors are in thrall to their machines, and many others are strikingly greedy, loading their patients up with as many drugs as they can get away with. Dentists are also expensive.

If you need help contact the TIC for advice about English-speaking doctors. If you need help at once, shout *'Tas' kete kuré!'* ('Help!') at the top of your voice.

Chinese herbal medicine is very popular among Japanese and can be remarkably efficacious for minor problems. Many ordinary-looking drugstores specialize in Chinese medicine, called *kanpo-yaku*. Acupuncture (*hari*) and finger-massage (*shiatsu*) are other Chinese-derived treatments which are popular. Practitioners are all licensed but far from cheap. The TIC may be able to help you find a good one.

Western medicines and drugs are available from the **American Pharmacy**, a short step from Tokyo's TIC.

CLOTHING

Short sleeves and cotton clothes for summer. Nobody likes wearing jackets in summer but most salarymen still do,

and if you are on business so should you. Casual wear is acceptable at all but a very few nightspots in the capital. Bring sweaters and a warm coat for winter. If you wear your souvenir happi coat you will cause great mirth, unless you are at a festival. Likewise with kimono, though at a *ryokan* it's all right to slop around in the *yukata* (informal kimono, also used for nightwear) you are issued with. Remember the left-hand

panel goes over the right for both men and women; the opposite way is only for corpses. Split-toed socks (*tabi*) are useful for *ryokan* in winter and go with the split-toed sandals. They make good

ABOVE Yokohama department store, BELOW Kamakura okonomiyaki house, with the ingredients displayed outside. OVERLEAF Imported goods shop in Yokohama's Chinatown.

souvenirs, too. Slip-on shoes -- no laces -- make life much easier at *ryokan* and private houses, where you are always taking them off and putting them on.

ESCORTS

Several escort services advertise in *Tour Companion.*

SHOPPING

Foreign tourists are allowed tax-free privileges on a range of goods, including cameras, audio and other electrical equipment, watches and pearls. This means a discount of between 10 and 20 per cent. A number of shops with the tourist in mind specialize in tax-free goods. These include the shopping arcades in the Imperial and Palace Hotels and the Sukiyabashi Shopping Center in Ginza.

When you're shopping tax-free remember to take your passport, and remind the assistant about the discount. Retain copies of the documents he gives you as you will have to surrender them to Customs on leaving Japan. Customs may also demand to see your purchases, or, failing that, mailing receipts to prove you have sent them on.

Discounts are only available on fairly pricey items but there are many other Japanese souvenirs the folks back home would appreciate: *tabi*, *geta*, *zori*, *jikatabi* (footwear), kimono and *obi* (sash), *jimbei* (two-piece summer lounging wear), silk, pottery, dolls, woodblock prints, paper umbrellas, bamboo ware, lacquer ware, tea-ceremony equipment, swords, knives, geisha wigs...

For your everyday needs use the many department stores. Foreign foods of all sorts are available at supermarkets such as the Olympia Foodliner in Roppongi and Kinokuniya in Aoyama. Japanese bread, at least that available in

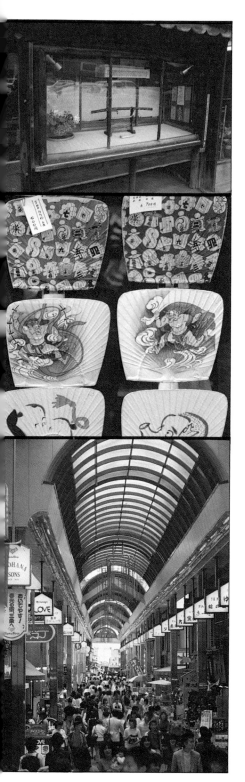

major cities, has improved enormously in the past ten years.

Details of stores that offer tax-free shopping may be found in *Tour Companion*.

TRAVELING

PLANES

The two major operators of domestic air services are All Nippon Airways and Toa Domestic Airlines. Call the numbers listed below for details of their services.

The following are the phone numbers of Tokyo's airline offices:

Aeroflot (03) 272-8351
Air Canada (03) 586-3891
Air France (03) 475-1511
Air India (03) 214-1981
Air New Zealand (03) 287-1641
Alitalia (03) 580-2181
All Nippon Airways (03) 580-4711
American Airlines (03) 212-0861
Austrian Airlines (03) 213-1751
British Airways (03) 214-4161
Canadian Pacific Air (03) 212-5811
Cathay Pacific Airways (03) 504-1531
China Airlines (03) 436-1661
Continental Air Micronesia (03) 592-1631
Egypt Air (03) 211-4521
Finn Air (03) 580-9231
Flying Tiger (03) 581-6841
Garuda Indonesian Airways (03) 593-1181
Iran Air (03) 586-2101
Iraqi Airways (03) 586-5801
Japan Air Lines (03) 457-1111
Japan Asia Airways (03) 455-7511

Souvenirs: OPPOSITE, TOP BOTTOM masks of Ebisu-sama, the merchants' cheerful divinity, fans, ceramic *tanuki* (raccoon dogs); ABOVE, TOP TO BOTTOM hand-smithied swords, hand-painted fans, and a typical covered shopping arcade.

KLM Royal Dutch Airlines (03) 216-0771
Korean Airlines (03) 211-3311
Lot Polish Airlines (03) 437-5741
Lufthansa German Airlines (03) 580-2111
Malaysian Airline System (03) 503-5961
Northwest Airlines (03) 433-8151
Olympic Airways (03) 583-6854
Pakistan International (03) 216-6511
Pan American World Airways (03) 240-8888
Philippine Airlines (03) 580-1571
Qantas Airways (03) 212-1351
Sabena (03) 585-6151

Scandinavia Airlines (03) 503-8101
Singapore Airlines (03) 213-3431
South African Airways (03) 470-1901
Swissair (03) 212-1016
Thai Airways International (03) 503-3311
Toa Domestic Airlines (03) 507-8030
Trans World Airlines (03) 212-8876
United Airlines (03) 213-4511
UTA French Airlines (03) 593-0773
Varig Brazilian Airlines (03) 211-6751
Western Airlines (03) 213-2777

RAILWAYS

The Japanese railway network is one

of the best and most comprehensive in the world. It's expensive, and Japanese National Railways (JNR) is losing money hand over fist, but the trains are fast, clean and very punctual. As the land area of Japan is not very large, and asroads are frequently clogged with cars, rail travel is the most attractive way for most visitors to see Japan.

JNR Services

The **Shinkansen** runs at maximum speeds of 210 k.p.h. (130 m.p.h.) be-

tween Tokyo and Hakata, by way of Nagoya, Kyoto, Osaka and Hiroshima. Two other services run north of the capital, one to Morioka in Iwate Prefecture and one to Niigata on the Japan Sea Coast.

Tokkyu trains (special express) are the fastest trains apart from the Shinkansen and are used for long-distance travel on other lines.

Kyuko trains (ordinary express) make a limited number of stops.

Futsu trains (ordinary) stop at all stations.

Fares are calculated according to distance. If you travel by any train other than a *futsu* you also have to pay a surcharge; extra is also charged for reserved seats. The Green Window (*Midori-no-madoguchi*) and Travel Service Centers at JNR stations sell these surcharge tickets, as well as berth tickets for sleeping cars.

A few representative Shinkansen fares:

Tokyo - Odawara: fare ¥1,310; surcharge for Shinkansen: ¥2,000.

Tokyo -- Kyoto: fare ¥7,100; surcharge ¥5,000.

Tokyo -- Hiroshima: fare ¥10,200; surcharge ¥6,400.

Tokyo -- Hakata: fare ¥12,100; surcharge ¥7,900.

Tokyo -- Niigata: fare ¥5,000; surcharge ¥4,200.

The surcharges shown here are for reserved seats. If an unreserved seat is used all the way the charge is ¥500 less.

The surcharge for Tokkyu trains is cheaper than for the Shinkansen, but the trip of course takes longer, and on lines that run parallel with Shinkansen services there are not many trains. A

very few Kyuko and Futsu trains cover long-distances overnight with no sleeping cars. It may be hard to sleep but these, along with JNR's bus service from Tokyo to Kyoto, are the cheapest ways of crossing the country.

A **Japan Rail Pass** can be bought outside Japan in two classes, Green or Ordinary. Green passes entitle the holder to travel in Green Cars (a euphemism for First Class). They run for 7, 14 or 21 days, and constitute a great saving if you plan to travel a lot. A 7-day ordinary pass costs ¥27,000; a 14-

day ordinary costs ¥43,000; and a 21-day ordinary, ¥55,000. You can use the pass to travel throughout Japan on JNR lines.

Excursion tickets, called *shuyuken*, can be economical if you plan to travel from Tokyo to a particular area, for example Kyushu, and travel around in that area for some days. The details of these tickets are complicated; ask the TIC to help, or take a Japanese-

OPPOSITE AND ABOVE Assorted bike riders and ABOVE LEFT a cluster of reason why driving in Japan can be a nightmare.

speaking friend to the station with you.

Timetables. The TIC have a Condensed Railway Timetable in English which gives details of all Shinkansen and some other main-line services and gives a good run-down on fares, facilities and other details. However, the ambitious traveler who plans to travel extensively in the country alone should arm himself with a copy of *Jikokuhyo*, the book of timetables, published monthly, which covers all the trains, buses, planes and ferries in the country. It's published in various editions, available at station kiosks, at a price of about ¥600. The drawback? It's all in Japanese!

However, with a good English-language map of Japan to compare with the maps in the front of *Jikokuhyo*, and with a lot of patience, it's possible to use this volume without any knowledge of the language. The numbers on the train and ferry lines marked on the map refer to the page on which the timetable for that particular service starts; the arrow next to the number shows the direction. You may spend an inordinate amount of the journey with your head buried in the timetable, but the feeling of satisfaction when you sort it out is immense!

BUSES

Local buses are hard to use because destinations are not written in roman letters.

There are three overnight 'Dream' buses from Tokyo, one each to Nagoya, Kyoto and Osaka. They are operated by JNR.

Nagoya bus: departs Tokyo 11.20 p.m., arrives Nagoya 6.01 a.m. Total cost: ¥6,000.

Kyoto bus: departs Tokyo 11 a.m., arrives Kyoto 7.45 a.m. Total cost: ¥7,800.

Osaka bus: departs Tokyo 10.20 p.m., arrives Osaka 7.40 a.m. Total cost: ¥8,200.

These buses leave from the Yaesu side of Tokyo station, near the south entrance. Tickets can be bought from the Travel Service Center nearby.

RENT-A-CAR SERVICES

In Japan they drive on the left. If you have a valid international driving permit you can rent a car, from **Nippon Rent-a-Car** (affiliated with Hertz) or one of several other companies. It is a very good idea to take a Japanese-speaking companion along with you, at least as far as the office: the clerks are not obliged to be able to speak English and will explain the details of liability in the case of accident and so on in Japanese.

If you can take your Japanese companion along for the whole trip, so much the better. There are very few romanized road signs in Japan -- the only consistent exception, a completely useless one, is the names of rivers -- and if you can't read the name of your destination and the various places en route in Chinese characters you stand a good chance of getting lost. If you are bent on traveling without native assistance get hold of two maps, one romanized and one in Japanese, and memorize the necessary characters in advance.

But even if you do your homework properly you will find that driving in Japan is an experience full of excitement and tension. Roads in the boondocks are astonishingly narrow, and the placing of road signs is uniformly haphazard. Furthermore, there are far too many cars crowding on to far too few decent roads, and away from the splendid expressways the traffic often crawls along.

Representative prices: compact Honda City, ¥6,000 per day; ten-seat van, ¥22,000 to ¥26,700 per day.

Nippon and Toyota car rental companies both have desks at Narita Airport. Nippon's phone number in Tokyo is (03) 496-0919; Toyota's is (03) 264-2834.

TAXIS

A taxi with a red light in the window is cruising for a fare. The door at the back on the left-hand side will open and close automatically (it is operated by the driver). Minimum fare is ¥470 at the moment, though it rises frequently. After the first two kilometers (1.6 miles) it will rise by an extra ¥80 for each 370 meters (405 yards) traveled. If you are stuck in traffic you pay for it, to the tune of ¥80 for every 15 seconds. The fare which registers on the meter is the total charge. Fares are 20 per cent higher between 11 p.m. and 5 a.m. Before using an expressway in Tokyo the driver will normally ask your permission as the toll, ¥500 for small cars, ¥1,000 for large ones, will go on your bill.

The days when it was common, early in the morning in Ginza, to come across taxis upside down with their wheels gently spinning, are fortunately over. Your driver still believes himself to be king of the road, however. If he's going too fast yell '*Yukkuri!*' ('Take it easy!')

HITCHHIKING

Proceed as in other countries. A bold sign with the name of your destination (in Chinese characters) is a great aid. Hitchhiking is not popular even with young people in Japan as it conflicts with the pervasive belief that a debt incurred should be repaid -- and it is difficult for a hitchhiker to repay his debt. Hitchers in Japan often find they are overwhelmed with kindness, with drivers going miles and even days out of their way.

THE LAST WORD

Two thousand years of alien history -- the crowds -- the typhoons -- the earthquakes -- you can't take it any more! If you're in Tokyo, phone **Tokyo English Life Line (TELL)** and talk to them

about it. 9 a.m. to 1 p.m. and 7 to 11 p.m. daily. Tel: (03) 264-4347.

INSTANT JAPANESE

Japanese is a swine to speak, but it's not hard to pronounce. So let's start with the easy bit.

Say the sentence, 'Pass me two egg rolls.' You have now spoken all the vowels of Japanese, and in the right order: a-i-u-e-o. The only modification

ABOVE Street cleaners at work in Yokohama.

203

we might make is to cut off the 'lls' of 'rolls' so the 'o' sound is short, as in the word 'hot'.

Consonants are easy too, roughly the same as English except for 'g' which is always hard and 'r' which is somewhere between 'r' and 'l'. The Japanese cannot in fact distinguish between the two sounds, which causes endless problems with words like 'pray', 'clap' and 'rice'.

A bar over a vowel lengthens it: 'kyu'

(abrupt) becomes 'kyuuu', for example; 'hot' becomes 'ho-o-ot' (not 'hoot').

Most Japanese words end with a vowel. This is why borrowed words sound strange. 'Beer' becomes '*beer-u*', 'baseball' becomes '*baseboor-u*', "hot' becomes '*hot-to*' and so on.

A few basic phrases will delight the Japanese because it means you are trying hard. Soon you will hear that great word '*jozu!*' ('skillful!') ringing in your ears.

Good morning. *O-ha-yo go-za-i-mas'*.

Good afternoon. *Kon-ni-chi-wa.*
Good evening. *Kon-ban-wa.*
Good night. *O-ya-su-mi-na-sai.*
Goodbye. *Sayonara.*
Yes. *Hai.*
No. *Ie.*
Beer, please. *Beeru ku-da-sai*
Coffee, please. *Kohi ku-da-sai.*
Menu, please. *Menu ku-da-sai.*
Thanks. *A-ri-ga-to.*
Thank you very much. *Do-mo a-ri-ga-to.*
That's all right. *Do i-ta-shi-ma-sh'te.*
It's wrong. *Chi-ga-i-ma-su.*
That's right. *So des'.*
I don't understand. *Wa-ka-ri-ma-sen.*
I understand. *Wa-ka-ri-ma-shi-ta.*
Please wait a minute.]*Chot-to-mat-te ku-da-sai.*
I'm sorry. *Su-mi-ma-sen.*
Thanks (in a shop). *Su-mi-ma-sen.*
Please (requesting something). *O-ne-gai-shi-ma-s'.*
Please take me to Tokyo station. *To-kyo eki ma-de o-ne-gai-shi-mas'.*

The most important point to bear in mind is that you should enunciate each syllable separately and distinctly, without slurring. We don't do this in English so it takes some practice. But relish the satisfaction of getting your point across!

If you want to study the language formally, schools advertise in the back of the *Japan Times*. One such in Tokyo, Sony LL (tel: 504-1356) claims that it can teach you to handle yourself in 'just about any daily situation' in 22 weeks.

Bibliography

KOBO ABE, *The Woman in the Dunes,* New York, Random House, 1972. Translated by E. Dale Saunders.

JAN BROWN, *Exploring Tohoku,* Tokyo, Weatherhill, 1983.

JAMES CLAVEL, *Shogun,* London, Hodder & Stoughton, 1975.

EUGENE HERRIGAL, *Zen in the Art of Archery,* London, Routledge & Kegan Paul, 1953.

MASUJIBUSE, *Black Rain,* Tokyo, Kodansha International, 1969. Translated by John Bester.

MATSUO BASHO, *The Narrow Road to the Deep North and Other Travel Sketches,* London, Penguin Books, 1966. Translated by Yuasa Nobuyuki.

-- --, *A Haiku Journey -- Basho's Narrow Road to a Far Province,* Tokyo, Kodansha International, 1974. Translated and introduced by Dorothy Britton.

YUKIO MISHIMA, *Five Modern Noh Plays,* New York, Alfred A. Knopf, 1957. Translated by Donald Keene.

MURASAKI SHIKIBU, *The Tale of Genji,* New York, Alfred A. Knopf, 1966. Translated by Edward G. Seidensticker.

DONALD RICHIE, *The Inland Sea,* Tokyo, Weatherhill, 1971.

R. STEVENS, *Kanazawa: The Other Side of Japan,* Kanazawa, Society to Introduce Kanazawa to the World, Kanazawa Chamber of Commerce, 1979.

YOUTH HOSTEL HANDBOOK, 1982 ed. Tokyo, Japan Youth Hostels Inc.

Index

210

INDEX TO PREFECTURES